GLOBALVIEWPOINTS

| Climate Change

Other Books of Related Interest:

Opposing Viewpoints Series

Endangered Oceans

At Issue Series

Greenhouse Gases

Current Controversies Series

Biodiversity

Global Warming

Introducing Issues with Opposing Viewpoints Series

Oil

GLOBALVIEWPOINTS

Climate Change

Adrienne Wilmoth Lerner and Chiara St. Pierre,
Book Editors

GREENHAVEN PRESS
A part of Gale, Cengage Learning

GALE
CENGAGE Learning™

Detroit • New York • San Francisco • New Haven, Conn • Waterville, Maine • London

Christine Nasso, *Publisher*
Elizabeth Des Chenes, *Managing Editor*

© 2009 Greenhaven Press, a part of Gale, Cengage Learning

Gale and Greenhaven Press are registered trademarks used herein under license.

For more information, contact:
Greenhaven Press
27500 Drake Rd.
Farmington Hills, MI 48331-3535
Or you can visit our Internet site at gale.cengage.com

Articles in Greenhaven Press anthologies are often edited for length to meet page requirements. In addition, original titles of these works are changed to clearly present the main thesis and to explicitly indicate the author's opinion. Every effort is made to ensure that Greenhaven Press accurately reflects the original intent of the authors. Every effort has been made to trace the owners of copyrighted material.

Cover Image copyright Armin Rose, 2008. Used under license from Shutterstock.com.

LIBRARY OF CONGRESS CATALOGING-IN-PUBLICATION DATA

Climate change / Adrienne Wilmoth Lerner and Chiara St. Pierre, book editors.
p. cm. -- (Global viewpoints)
Includes bibliographical references and index.
ISBN 978-0-7377-4156-8 (hardcover)
ISBN 978-0-7377-4157-5 (pbk.)
1. Global temperature changes--Popular works. 2. Global environmental changes--Popular works. 3. Climatic changes--Popular works. I. Lerner, Adrienne Wilmoth. II. St. Pierre, Chiara.
QC903. C44 2009
363.738'74--dc22
2008048355

Printed in the United States of America
1 2 3 4 5 6 7 13 12 11 10 09

8|09

Contents

Foreword   11

Introduction   14

World Map   18

Chapter 1: Debating Global Climate Change

1. International Science Societies Concur That   20
   Climate Change Is Happening
   RoyalSociety.org
   The professional science societies of several nations—
   Brazil, Canada, China, France, Germany, India, Italy,
   Japan, Russia, United Kingdom, and the United
   States—declare that "climate change is real" and ask
   policy makers to address climate change issues.

2. Nobel Committee Recognizes Climate Change   26
   Scientists and Advocates
   R.K. Pachauri
   The 2007 Nobel Peace Prize lecture, given by R.K.
   Pachauri of the United Nations Intergovernmental Panel
   on Climate Change, highlights the scientific consensus
   that human activity is changing Earth's climate.

3. World's Scientists Acknowledge Uncertainties   41
   and Disagreements, but Most Agree Climate
   Change Is a Real Threat
   Fred Pearce
   A significant majority of the world's climate scientists
   agree that climate change is happening, but many
   researchers disagree about its progression and impacts. A
   slim minority disputes this core scientific consensus and
   denies the existence of human-driven climate change.

4. Climate Change Skeptics Do Not Receive   **51**
Equal Funding
Jeff Mason

Scientists espousing varying degrees of climate change skepticism claim it is difficult to obtain funding for their research, especially from European governments and organizations.

5. **European Union** Nations Assert That   **55**
Policies of the United States Fail to Address
Climate Change
Markus Becker and Holger Dambeck

European nations accuse the United States, one of the world's top emitters of greenhouse gases, of having an irresponsible policy on climate change. European Union countries wanted the United States to join the existing Kyoto Protocol and agree to discuss and enact future emissions reduction targets.

6. **United Kingdom** Research Group Asserts That   **62**
Climate Change May Benefit Humans
Antony Barnett and Mark Townsend

Environmentalists oppose a corporate-funded British policy group that asserts that human-induced climate change may not exist.

7. **United States** Congress Alleges Federal   **67**
Interference with Climate Change Science
United States House of Representatives, Committee on Oversight and Government Reform

Responding to allegations in the international media, the U.S. House Oversight Committee investigated federal executive and agency policies on climate change science, asserting that federal staff censored and deliberately disregarded scientific work on climate change issues.

Periodical Bibliography   **73**

Chapter 2: The Impact of Global Climate Change

1. The International Economic Impacts of   75
   Climate Change: An Overview
   Nicholas Stern
   From adopting new farming practices to relocating
   population centers, an organization tries to assess the
   potential economic costs of global climate change.

2. **Malawi**'s Food Security Is Threatened   83
   by Climate Change
   Singy Hanyona
   Climate change and a lack of agricultural adaptation are
   causing food scarcity in southern African nations already
   burdened by high rates of drought and disease.

3. The **Middle East** Faces Water Shortages   90
   and Food Scarcity Due to Climate Change
   *United Nations Office for the Coordination
   of Humanitarian Affairs*
   Climate change threatens food security throughout the
   region, but Yemen—already struggling with water
   shortages—will likely be the nation most severely
   affected. Observers worry that scarcity of food, water,
   and farming land could trigger political and social
   unrest in the region.

4. **Bangladeshis** Fear Climate Change Will Bring   96
   Stronger Storms, Flooding, and Famine
   Fred de Sam Lazaro
   Bangladeshis worry that rising sea levels may destroy
   farms and villages, increase salt levels in soil and fresh
   water, and force millions of people to flee to crowded
   cities. Climate change may also strengthen the seasonal
   monsoons and cyclones that lash the region.

5. Small Island States Face Substantial
   Challenges from Rising Sea Levels
   Intergovernmental Panel on Climate Change:
   Working Group II
   Rising sea levels threaten the future of small island
   states, especially in the South Pacific region. Food and
   water shortages and land scarcity may ultimately lead to
   the abandonment of some islands.

103

6. **South America**'s Amazon Basin Faces Loss
   of Animal Species and Habitats
   Michael Case
   The Amazon rain forests are home to millions of plant
   and animal species unique to the region. However,
   deforestation and climate change could cause many
   species—and the rain forests themselves—to become
   extinct.

109

7. **Canada**'s Inuit Peoples Are Affected
   by Arctic Melting
   Emily Gertz
   Inuit groups in Canada view combating arctic melting
   and global warming as human rights issues. For the
   Inuit, whose traditions depend on a thriving tundra,
   retreating ice caps and environmental degradation may
   undermine their communities.

135

8. **Italy**'s Canal City of Venice Must Cope
   with Rising Sea Levels
   Eric Jaffe
   A new floodgate system is designed to spare Venice,
   Italy, from regular flooding, but it will fail to protect the
   city from rising sea levels.

144

Periodical Bibliography

150

Chapter 3: Developing Nations and Climate Change

1. Climate Change Disproportionately Affects the   152
   Inhabitants of Developing Nations
   Rachel Oliver

   Environmental justice advocates assert that the world's poorest citizens produce the fewest greenhouse gas emissions but are more likely to feel the most severe impacts of climate change.

2. Poor Nations Must Also Work to Cut   159
   Carbon Emissions
   Haider Rizvi

   Developing nations in the global South should work to reduce their own emissions, whether or not they receive funds for "green" projects from the world's wealthiest nations.

3. International Emissions Restrictions May   165
   Harm Developing Regions
   Hans Martin Seip and Sigbjorn Gronas

   Researchers consider whether emissions restrictions in industrialized nations may hinder economic growth in the world's developing regions and contribute to poverty.

4. **China**'s Rapid Development Raises Global   170
   Levels of Greenhouse Gas Emissions
   The Economist

   Rapid development in China is causing the nation's greenhouse gas emissions to soar above scientific estimates as the nation constructs new coal-burning power plants to meet its increased energy needs.

Periodical Bibliography   181

Chapter 4: Combating Global Climate Change

1. Worldwide Tree Planting Project Aims   **183**
   to Offset Some Emissions
   United Nations Environment Programme

   The United Nations Environment Programme launches
   a successful campaign to plant a billion trees in an effort
   to fight climate change. The project is intended to
   alleviate desertification and deforestation as well as
   offset carbon emissions.

2. Information Technology Companies Can   **193**
   Take Action Against Climate Change
   Michael Dell

   The founder of a large international corporation asserts
   that both national policies and individual commitments
   to "green" living are essential to combating climate
   change.

3. **Australia**'s Government Bans Traditional   **199**
   Light Bulbs
   Wendy Frew and Linton Besser

   Australia bans traditional incandescent light bulbs in
   favor of energy-wise compact fluorescent lights.

4. **Philippine** Activists Protest Construction   **204**
   of a Coal-Fired Power Plant
   Greenpeace

   Environmental activists from Greenpeace International
   and local citizens gather to protest the construction of a
   power plant in Iliolo, Philippines. The protestors oppose
   the plant's use of coal and lack of emissions-reducing
   technology.

Periodical Bibliography   **208**

For Further Discussion   **209**

Glossary   **211**

Organizations to Contact   **216**

Bibliography of Books   **219**

Index   **223**

Foreword

Global interdependence has become an undeniable reality. Mass media and technology have increased worldwide access to information and created a society of global citizens. Understanding and navigating this global community is a challenge, requiring a high degree of information literacy and a new level of learning sophistication.

Building on the success of its flagship series, *Opposing Viewpoints*, Greenhaven Press has created the *Global Viewpoints* series to examine a broad range of current, often controversial topics of worldwide importance from a variety of international perspectives. Providing students and other readers with the information they need to explore global connections and think critically about worldwide implications, each *Global Viewpoints* volume offers a panoramic view of a topic of widespread significance.

Drugs, famine, immigration—a broad, international treatment is essential to do justice to social, environmental, health, and political issues such as these. Junior high, high school, and early college students, as well as general readers, can all use *Global Viewpoints* anthologies to discern the complexities relating to each issue. Readers will be able to examine unique national perspectives while, at the same time, appreciating the interconnectedness that global priorities bring to all nations and cultures.

Material in each volume is selected from a diverse range of sources, including journals, magazines, newspapers, nonfiction books, speeches, government documents, pamphlets, organization newsletters, and position papers. *Global Viewpoints* is truly global, with material drawn primarily from international sources available in English and secondarily from U.S. sources with extensive international coverage.

Features of each volume in the *Global Viewpoints* series include:

- An **annotated table of contents** that provides a brief summary of each essay in the volume, including the name of the country or area covered in the essay.

- An **introduction** specific to the volume topic.

- A **world map** to help readers locate the countries or areas covered in the essays.

- For each viewpoint, an **introduction** that contains notes about the author and source of the viewpoint explains why material from the specific country is being presented, summarizes the main points of the viewpoint, and offers three **guided reading questions** to aid in understanding and comprehension.

- **For further discussion** questions that promote critical thinking by asking the reader to compare and contrast aspects of the viewpoints or draw conclusions about perspectives and arguments.

- A worldwide list of **organizations to contact** for readers seeking additional information.

- A **periodical bibliography** for each chapter and a **bibliography of books** on the volume topic to aid in further research.

- A comprehensive **subject index** to offer access to people, places, events, and subjects cited in the text, with the countries covered in the viewpoints highlighted.

Global Viewpoints is designed for a broad spectrum of readers who want to learn more about current events, history, political science, government, international relations, economics, environmental science, world cultures, and sociology—students doing research for class assignments or debates, teachers and faculty seeking to supplement course materials, and others wanting to understand current issues better. By presenting how people in various countries perceive the root causes, current consequences, and proposed solutions to worldwide challenges, *Global Viewpoints* volumes offer readers opportunities to enhance their global awareness and their knowledge of cultures worldwide.

Introduction

"Climate change is real. The science is compelling. And the longer we wait, the harder the problem will be to solve.

—*John Kerry,*
United States Senator

Human activities alter Earth's climate. From farming to driving, industrial production to power generation, human actions produce pollutants with the power to warm global temperatures, melt polar ice caps, change the oceans, and alter average weather patterns worldwide. Deserts may expand, taking over land once used for agriculture. Coastal populations worldwide face significant challenges from inundation by rising seas. Some of the anticipated effects of global climate change may take generations to realize, others—such as the retreat of polar ice—are already happening.

In 1896, researchers first proposed that industrial emissions from industrial plants burning fossil fuels could raise Earth's average temperature. This basic idea was developed over time, eventually leading to present-day models of global warming. In the 1930s, researchers compiled data on average temperatures in the northeastern part of the United States that they asserted showed a rapid warming trend. However, most scientists at the time attributed the findings to a natural warming cycle, noting that Earth's geological record of its climate evidenced numerous shifts through the ages.

In the 1950s, researchers developed the first models demonstrating the potential warming properties of built-up carbon dioxide and other pollutants in the atmosphere. By 1962, researchers proved that atmospheric levels of gases were rising. The predicted warming trend became known as the "greenhouse effect." The worldwide rise of the environmental movement in the late 1960s brought popular attention to scientific research on global warming. More universities and national governments invested in climate research.

Over the following decade, many new theories of climate change developed. Along with global warming, some researchers asserted that human activity and industrialization could initiate a period of global cooling as pollutants prevented solar radiation from adequately warming the earth's surface. Other researchers noted that the greenhouse effect was always present, radiating lost heat back to Earth's surface and keeping surface temperatures more temperate and stable. However, human activity intensified the greenhouse effect, potentially accelerating warming. The first models were developed showing potential concerns from changing ocean currents and sea level rise.

During the late-1970s through 2000, researchers, governments, and individuals began to recognize and address climate issues. After researchers discovered that harmful aerosols that contained chlorofluorocarbons (CFCs) were depleting the ozone layer, the issues of global warming and the "Ozone Hole"—spots of Earth's ozone layer over the poles that showed significant depletion—gained international media attention. The Montreal Protocol, a 1987 international ban on harmful aerosols, successfully stemmed rapid ozone depletion. It also provided a foundation for nations to work cooperatively to address climate issues. A decade later, many nations adopted the Kyoto Protocol, an agreement to reduce or limit their greenhouse gas emissions.

By 2001, the United Nations Intergovernmental Panel on Climate Change (IPCC), charged with compiling and evaluating worldwide scientific climate research, declared in its annual report that it was "much more likely than not" that Earth faced global warming and that human activity was accelerating its onset. In 2007, the Intergovernmental Panel on Climate

Change reported that research indicated a probable global temperature rise of 3°F to 7.2°F (1.8°–4°C) by the turn of the next century.

Global warming is the most popularly known aspect of climate change. However, it is only one of many probable climate issues identified by researchers. Climate scientists and policy makers now advocate the term "global climate change" because it covers a diversity of climate issues. Global climate change refers inclusively to all human-influenced climate issues. Instead of focusing only on warming, the term global climate change draws attention to climate challenges such as drought, food and freshwater scarcity, sea level rise, changing ocean currents, emissions, and ozone layer depletion. Global climate change also includes seemingly disparate models of change.

A significant majority of the world's scientists now acknowledge that human actions contribute to climate change. While there are many competing models of climate change and healthy disagreement over the scale of some of its effects, current climate science holds that climate change is happening. Disagreements over the rate of polar ice retreat or the possible height of peak sea level rise do not undermine the validity of global climate change as a scientific theory. Rather, they are part of the rigorous scientific process that tests and assesses scientific hypotheses. In other words, climate researchers know that human actions affect climate, but are trying to see how much those actions could change Earth.

Though there is a scientific consensus on climate change, there is no political consensus on the issue. Many national leaders—especially members of the European Union—support large-scale international treaties with reduction plans for greenhouse gas emissions, such as the Kyoto Protocol. The United States traditionally opposes international agreements with binding emissions reduction goals. U.S. policy makers assert that binding agreements may harm national economic development and that any effective treaty must place emissions reduction requirements on large developing nations such as China and India. Many developing nations assert that the current climate threat was created by the world's large industrial powers and therefore those countries should take the most responsibility in addressing climate change. Leaders in developing nations maintain that they must have the ability to address national health and economic problems before spending money on climate change abatement and that wealthy nations should aid developing nations by funding environmental projects. However, many developing nations also participate in international climate change treaties and programs. A majority of the world's nations agree on the basic premise that something must be done to immediately address climate change issues.

GLOBALVIEWPOINTS

CHAPTER 1

Debating Global Climate Change

International Science Societies Concur That Climate Change Is Happening

RoyalSociety.org

"Climate change is real," proclaims the Joint Statement issued by several nations' leading science associations. The science academies produced the Joint Statement to legitimize and encourage climate change research. The statement challenges national governments to enact scientifically informed policies that will counteract human-induced climate change. The Joint Statement was first signed and adopted by eleven of the world's leading national science organizations.

As you read, consider the following questions:

1. On average, how many degrees cooler would Earth's temperatures be if greenhouse gases were not present in the atmosphere?
2. Over the next twenty-five years, the world's estimated energy demands are expected to increase by how much?
3. The Intergovernmental Panel on Climate Change estimates that the global mean sea level will rise between 0.1 and 0.9 meters from 1990–2100. What are the two combined reasons for this rise?

There will always be uncertainty in understanding a system as complex as the world's climate. However, there is now strong evidence that significant global warming is occurring. The evidence comes from direct measurements of rising surface air temperatures and subsurface ocean temperatures and from phenomena such as increases in average global sea levels, retreating glaciers, and changes to many physical and biological systems. It is likely that most of the warming in recent decades can be attributed to human activities. This warming has already led to changes in the earth's climate.

The existence of greenhouse gases in the atmosphere is vital to life on Earth—in their absence average temperatures would be about 30 centigrade degrees lower than they are today. But human activities are now causing atmospheric concentrations of greenhouse gases—including carbon dioxide, methane, tropospheric ozone, and nitrous oxide—to rise well above pre-industrial levels. Carbon dioxide levels have increased from 280 ppm [parts per million] in 1750 to over 375 ppm today—higher than any previous levels that can be reliably measured (i.e., in the last 420,000 years). Increasing greenhouse gases are causing temperatures to rise; the earth's surface warmed by approximately 0.6 centigrade degrees over the 20th century. The Intergovernmental Panel on Climate Change (IPCC) projected that the average global surface temperatures will continue to increase to between 1.4 centigrade degrees and 5.8 centigrade degrees above 1990 levels, by 2100.

Even with possible lowered emission rates we will be experiencing the impacts of climate change throughout the 21st century and beyond.

Reduce the Causes of Climate Change

The scientific understanding of climate change is now sufficiently clear to justify nations taking prompt action. It is vital that all nations identify cost-effective steps that they can take now, to contribute to substantial and long-term reduction in net global greenhouse gas emissions.

Action taken now to reduce significantly the build-up of greenhouse gases in the atmosphere will lessen the magnitude and rate of climate change. As the United Nations Framework Convention on Climate Change (UNFCCC) recognises, a lack of full scientific certainty about some aspects of climate change is not a reason for delaying an immediate response that will, at a reasonable cost, prevent dangerous anthropogenic [caused by humans] interference with the climate system.

As nations and economies develop over the next 25 years, world primary energy demand is estimated to increase by almost 60%. Fossil fuels, which are responsible for the majority of carbon dioxide emissions produced by human activities, provide valuable resources for many nations and are projected to provide 85% of this demand. Minimising the amount of this carbon dioxide reaching the atmosphere presents a huge challenge. There are many potentially cost-effective technological options that could contribute to stabilizing greenhouse gas concentrations. These are at various stages of research and development. However, barriers to their broad deployment still need to be overcome.

Carbon dioxide can remain in the atmosphere for many decades. Even with possible lowered emission rates, we will be experiencing the impacts of climate change throughout the 21st century and beyond. Failure to implement significant reductions in net greenhouse gas emissions now will make the job much harder in the future.

Prepare for the Consequences of Climate Change

Major parts of the climate system respond slowly to changes in greenhouse gas concentrations. Even if greenhouse gas emissions were stabilised instantly at today's levels, the climate would still continue to change as it adapts to the increased

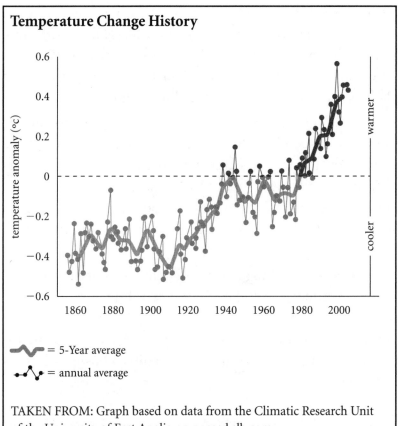

Temperature Change History

= 5-Year average

= annual average

TAKEN FROM: Graph based on data from the Climatic Research Unit of the University of East Anglia. www.seed.slb.com.

emission of recent decades. Further changes in climate are therefore unavoidable. Nations must prepare for them.

The projected changes in climate will have both beneficial and adverse effects at the regional level, for example on water resources, agriculture, natural ecosystems and human health. The larger and faster the changes in climate, the more likely it is that adverse effects will dominate. Increasing temperatures are likely to increase the frequency and severity of weather events such as heat waves and heavy rainfall. Increasing temperatures could lead to large-scale effects such as melting of large ice sheets (with major impacts on low-lying regions throughout the world). The IPCC estimates that the combined effects of ice melting and sea water expansion from ocean warming are projected to cause the global mean sea-level to rise by between 0.1 and 0.9 metres between 1990 and 2100. In Bangladesh alone, a 0.5 metre sea-level rise would place about 6 million people at risk from flooding.

Developing nations that lack the infrastructure or resources to respond to the impacts of climate change will be particularly affected. It is clear that many of the world's poorest people are likely to suffer the most from climate change. Long-term global efforts to create a more healthy, prosperous and sustainable world may be severely hindered by changes in the climate.

The task of devising and implementing strategies to adapt to the consequences of climate change will require worldwide collaborative input from a wide range of experts, including physical and natural scientists, engineers, social scientists, medical scientists, those in the humanities, business leaders and economists.

Prompt Action Is Needed

We urge all nations, in line with the UNFCCC principles, to take prompt action to reduce the causes of climate change, adapt to its impacts and ensure that the issue is included in all relevant national and international strategies. As national science academies, we commit to working with governments to help develop and implement the national and international response to the challenge of climate change.

G8 nations [the Group of Eight, a forum of developed countries] have been responsible for much of the past greenhouse gas emissions. As parties to the UNFCCC, G8 nations are committed to showing leadership in addressing climate change and assisting developing nations to meet the challenges of adaptation and mitigation.

We call on world leaders, including those meeting at the Gleneagles [Scotland] G8 Summit in July 2005, to:

- Acknowledge that the threat of climate change is clear and increasing.

- Launch an international study to explore scientifically informed targets for atmospheric greenhouse gas concentrations, and their associated emissions scenarios, that will enable nations to avoid impacts deemed unacceptable.

- Identify cost-effective steps that can be taken now to contribute to substantial and long-term reduction in net global greenhouse gas emissions. Recognise that delayed action will increase the risk of adverse environmental effects and will likely incur a greater cost.

- Work with developing nations to build a scientific and technological capacity best suited to their circumstances, enabling them to develop innovative solutions to mitigate and adapt to the adverse effects of climate change, while explicitly recognising their legitimate development rights.

- Show leadership in developing and deploying clean energy technologies and approaches to energy efficiency, and share this knowledge with all other nations.

- Mobilise the science and technology community to enhance research and development efforts, which can better inform climate change decisions.

Nobel Committee Recognizes Climate Change Scientists and Advocates

R.K. Pachauri

In 2007, the Norwegian Nobel Committee awarded the annual Nobel Peace Prize to the Intergovernmental Panel on Climate Change (IPCC) and former United States Vice President Al Gore. The recipients received the prize for their efforts to bring scientific and public awareness to climate change issues. In its Nobel Lecture, akin to an acceptance speech, given by R.K. Pachauri, chairman of the IPCC, the group outlined the most pressing effects of climate change and congratulated the work of international climate change researchers. The IPCC lecture presents climate change as a comprehensive threat to the world's human and animal populations, ecosystems, cultures, and economic systems. The IPCC is a United Nations organization dedicated to collecting and assessing international scientific research on climate change. The organization issues reports intended to inform policy makers worldwide.

As you read, consider the following questions:

1. Climate change will have several implications as well as adverse impacts for some populations. List three of the five areas affected by climate change.

R.K. Pachauri, Nobel Lecture, December 10, 2007. www.nobelprize.org. Copyright © The Nobel Foundation, Stockholm, 2007. Reproduced by permission.

2. How many species are expected to be at risk of extinction if global temperatures increase by 1.5–2.5 degrees Celsius?

3. In order to stabilize carbon dioxide emissions and limit global warming to 2 degrees Celsius, between what years must carbon dioxide emissions peak and then begin to decline?

Your Majesties, Your Royal Highnesses, Honourable Members of the Norwegian Nobel Committee, Excellencies, My Colleagues from the IPCC, Distinguished Ladies & Gentlemen.

As Chair of the Intergovernmental Panel on Climate Change (IPCC) I am deeply privileged to present this lecture on behalf of the Panel on the occasion of the Nobel Peace Prize being awarded to the IPCC jointly with Mr Al Gore. While doing so, I pay tribute to the thousands of experts and scientists who have contributed to the work of the Panel over almost two decades of exciting evolution and service to humanity. On this occasion, I also salute the leadership provided by my predecessors Prof. Bert Bolin and Dr Robert Watson. One of the major strengths of the IPCC is the procedures and practices that it has established over the years, and the credit for these go primarily to Prof. Bolin for their introduction and to Dr Watson for building on the efforts of the former most admirably. My gratitude also to UNEP [United Nations Environment Programme] and WMO [World Meteorological Organization] for their support, represented here today by Dr Mostapha Tolba and Dr Michel Jarraud respectively.

The Fourth Assessment Report of the IPCC has had a major impact in creating public awareness on various aspects of climate change, and the three Working Group reports as part of this assessment represent a major advance in scientific knowledge, for which I must acknowledge the remarkable leadership of the Co-Chairs of the three Working Groups: Dr

Susan Solomon [and] Dr Qin Dahe for Working Group I; Dr Martin Parry and Dr Osvaldo Canziani for Working Group II; and Dr Bert Metz and Dr Ogunlade Davidson for Working Group III, respectively. The Synthesis Report, which distills and integrates the major findings from these three reports has also benefited enormously from their valuable input.

The IPCC produces key scientific material that is of the highest relevance to policy making, and is agreed word-by-word by all governments, from the most skeptical to the most confident. This difficult process is made possible by the tremendous strength of the underlying scientific and technical material included in the IPCC reports.

In recent years several groups have studied the link between climate and security. These have raised the threat of dramatic population migration, conflict, and war over water and other resources as well as a realignment of power among nations.

The Panel was established in 1988 through a resolution of the UN [United Nations] General Assembly. One of its clauses was significant in having stated, "Noting with concern that the emerging evidence indicates that continued growth in atmospheric concentrations of 'greenhouse' gases could produce global warming with an eventual rise in sea levels, the effects of which could be disastrous for mankind if timely steps are not taken at all levels." This means that almost two decades ago the UN was acutely conscious of the possibility of disaster consequent on climate change through increases in sea levels. Today we know much more, which provides greater substance to that concern.

This award being given to the IPCC, we believe goes fundamentally beyond a concern for the impacts of climate change on peace. Mr Berge Furre expressed eloquently during the Nobel Banquet on 10 December 2004 an important tenet when he said, "We honour the earth; for bringing forth flowers and food—and trees . . . The Norwegian Nobel Committee is committed to the protection of the earth. This commitment is our vision—deeply felt and connected to human rights and peace". Honouring the IPCC through the grant of the Nobel Peace Prize in 2007 in essence can be seen as a clarion call for the protection of the earth as it faces the widespread impacts of climate change. The choice of the Panel for this signal honour is, in our view, an acknowledgement of three important realities, which can be summed up as:

1. The power and promise of collective scientific endeavour, which, as demonstrated by the IPCC, can reach across national boundaries and political differences in the pursuit of objectives defining the larger good of human society.

2. The importance of the role of knowledge in shaping public policy and guiding global affairs for the sustainable development of human society.

3. An acknowledgement of the threats to stability and human security inherent in the impacts of a changing climate and, therefore, the need for developing an effective rationale for timely and adequate action to avoid such threats in the future.

These three realities encircle an important truth that must guide global action involving the entire human race in the future. Coming as I do from India, a land which gave birth to civilization in ancient times and where much of the earlier tradition and wisdom guides actions even in modern times, the philosophy of "Vasudhaiva Kutumbakam", which means the whole universe is one family, must dominate global efforts to protect the global commons. This principle is crucial to the maintenance of peace and order today as it would be increasingly in the years ahead, and as the well-known columnist and author Thomas Friedman has highlighted in his book *The World is Flat.*

Impact of Climate Change

Neglect in protecting our heritage of natural resources could prove extremely harmful for the human race and for all species that share common space on planet earth. Indeed, there are many lessons in human history which provide adequate warning about the chaos and destruction that could take place if we remain guilty of myopic indifference to the progressive erosion and decline of nature's resources. Much has been written, for instance, about the Maya civilization, which flourished during 250–950 AD, but collapsed largely as a result of serious and prolonged drought. Even earlier, some 4000 years ago, a number of well-known Bronze Age cultures also crumbled extending from the Mediterranean to the Indus Valley, including the civilizations, which had blossomed in Mesopotamia. More recent examples of societies that collapsed or faced chaos on account of depletion or degradation of natural resources include the Khmer Empire in South East Asia, Easter Island, and several others. Changes in climate have historically determined periods of peace as well as conflict. The recent work of David Zhang has, in fact, highlighted the link between temperature fluctuations, reduced agricultural production, and the frequency of warfare in Eastern China over the last millennium. Further, in recent years several groups have studied the link between climate and security. These have raised the threat of dramatic population migration, conflict, and war over water and other resources as well as a realignment of power among nations. Some also highlight the possibility of rising tensions between rich and poor nations, health problems caused particularly by water shortages, and crop failures as well as concerns over nuclear proliferation.

One of the most significant aspects of the impacts of climate change, which has unfortunately not received adequate attention from scholars in the social sciences, relates to the equity implications of changes that are occurring and are likely to occur in the future. In general, the impacts of climate change on some of the poorest and the most vulnerable communities in the world could prove extremely unsettling. And, given the inadequacy of capacity, economic strength, and institutional capabilities characterizing some of these communities, they would remain extremely vulnerable to the impacts of climate change and may, therefore, actually see a decline in their economic condition, with a loss of livelihoods and opportunities to maintain even subsistence levels of existence. Since the IPCC by its very nature is an organization that does not provide assessments, which are policy prescriptive, it has not provided any directions on how conflicts inherent in the social implications of the impacts of climate change could be avoided or contained. Nevertheless, the Fourth Assessment Report provides scientific findings that other scholars can study and arrive at some conclusions on in relation to peace and security. Several parts of our reports have much information and knowledge that would be of considerable value for individual researchers and think tanks dealing with security issues as well as governments that necessarily are concerned with some of these matters. It would be particularly relevant to conduct in-depth analysis of risks to security among the most vulnerable sectors and communities impacted by climate change across the globe.

Peace can be defined as security and the secure access to resources that are essential for living. A disruption in such access could prove disruptive of peace. In this regard, climate change will have several implications, as numerous adverse impacts are expected for some populations in terms of:

- access to clean water

- access to sufficient food

- stable health conditions

- ecosystem resources

- security of settlements

Climate change is expected to exacerbate current stresses on water resources. On a regional scale, mountain snowpack, glaciers, and small ice caps play a crucial role in fresh water availability. Widespread mass losses from glaciers and reductions in snow cover over recent decades are projected to accelerate throughout the 21st century, reducing water availability, hydropower potential, and the changing seasonality of flows in regions supplied by meltwater from major mountain ranges (e.g. Hindu-Kush, Himalaya, Andes), where more than one-sixth of the world's population currently lives. There is also high confidence that many semi-arid areas (e.g. the Mediterranean Basin, western United States, southern Africa, and northeastern Brazil) will suffer a decrease in water resources due to climate change. In Africa by 2020, between 75 and 250 million people are projected to be exposed to increased water stress due to climate change.

In Africa by 2020, between 75 and 250 million people are projected to be exposed to increased water stress due to climate change.

Climate change could further adversely affect food security and exacerbate malnutrition at low latitudes, especially in seasonally dry and tropical regions, where crop productivity is projected to decrease for even small local temperature increases (1–2°C). By 2020, in some African countries, yields from rain-fed agriculture could be reduced by up to 50%. Agricultural production, including access to food, in many African countries is projected to be severely compromised.

The health status of millions of people is projected to be affected through, for example, increases in malnutrition; increased deaths, diseases, and injury due to extreme weather events; increased burden of diarrhoeal diseases; increased frequency of cardio-respiratory diseases due to higher concentrations of ground-level ozone in urban areas related to climate change; and the altered spatial distribution of some infectious diseases.

Regions Affected by Climate Change

Climate change is likely to lead to some irreversible impacts on biodiversity. There is medium confidence that approximately 20%–30% of species assessed so far are likely to be at increased risk of extinction if increases in global average warming exceed 1.5–2.5°C, relative to 1980–99. As global average temperature exceeds about 3.5°C, model projections suggest significant extinctions (40%–70% of species assessed) around the globe. These changes, if they were to occur would have serious effects on the sustainability of several ecosystems and the services they provide to human society.

As far as security of human settlements is concerned, vulnerabilities to climate change are generally greater in certain high-risk locations, particularly coastal and riverine areas, and areas whose economies are closely linked with climate-sensitive resources. Where extreme weather events become more intense or more frequent with climate change, the economic and social costs of those events will increase.

Some regions are likely to be especially affected by climate change.

- The Arctic, because of the impacts of high rates of projected warming on natural systems and human communities

- Africa, because of low adaptive capacity and projected climate change impacts

- Small islands, where there is high exposure of population and infrastructure to projected climate change impacts

Former United States Vice President Al Gore Shares Nobel Peace Prize with IPCC

So today, we dumped another 70 million tons of global-warming pollution into the thin shell of atmosphere surrounding our planet, as if it were an open sewer. And tomorrow, we will dump a slightly larger amount, with the cumulative concentrations now trapping more and more heat from the sun.

As a result, the earth has a fever. And the fever is rising. The experts have told us it is not a passing affliction that will heal by itself. We asked for a second opinion. And a third. And a fourth. And the consistent conclusion, restated with increasing alarm, is that something basic is wrong.

We are what is wrong, and we must make it right.

Al Gore, Nobel Lecture, December 10, 2007.
http://nobelprize.org.

- Asian and African mega-deltas, due to large populations and high exposure to sea level rise, storm surges, and river flooding

The IPCC Fourth Assessment Report concludes that non-climate stresses can increase vulnerability to climate change by reducing resilience and can also reduce adaptive capacity because of resource deployment towards competing needs. Vulnerable regions face multiple stresses that affect their exposure and sensitivity to various impacts as well as their capacity to adapt. These stresses arise from, for example, current climate hazards, poverty, and unequal access to resources, food insecurity, trends in economic globalization, conflict, and incidence of diseases such as HIV/AIDS.

Within other areas, even those with high incomes, some people (such as the poor, young children, and the elderly) can be particularly at risk.

Another issue of extreme concern is the finding that anthropogenic factors [those caused by humans] could lead to some impacts that are abrupt or irreversible, depending on the rate and magnitude of climate change.

Migration and movement of people is a particularly critical source of potential conflict. Migration, usually temporary and often from rural to urban areas, is a common response to calamities such as floods and famines. But as in the case of vulnerability to the impacts of climate change, where multiple stresses could be at work on account of a diversity of causes and conditions, so also in the case of migration, individuals may have multiple motivations and they could be displaced by multiple factors.

Another issue of extreme concern is the finding that anthropogenic factors [caused by humans] could lead to some impacts that are abrupt or irreversible, depending on the rate and magnitude of climate change. For instance, partial loss of ice sheets on polar land could imply metres of sea level rise, major changes in coastlines, and inundation of low-lying areas, with greatest effects in river deltas and low-lying islands.

Global average warming above about 4.5°C relative to 1980–99 (about 5°C above pre-industrial) would imply:

- Projected decreases of precipitation by up to 20% in many dry tropical and subtropical areas

- Expected mass loss of Greenland's ice if sustained over many centuries (based on all current global climate system models assessed) leading to sea level rise up to 4 metres and flooding of shorelines on every continent

The implications of these changes, if they were to occur would be grave and disastrous. However, it is within the reach of human society to meet these threats. The impacts of climate change can be limited by suitable adaptation measures and stringent mitigation of greenhouse gas emissions.

Society's Adaptation to Climate Change

Societies have a long record of adapting to the impacts of weather and climate. But climate change poses novel risks often outside the range of experience, such as impacts related to drought, heat waves, accelerated glacier retreat, and hurricane intensity. These impacts will require adaptive responses such as investments in storm protection and water supply infrastructure, as well as community health services. Adaptation measures essential to reduce such vulnerability, are seldom undertaken in response to climate change alone but can be integrated within, for example, water resource management, coastal defence, and risk-reduction strategies. The global community needs to coordinate a far more proactive effort towards implementing adaptation measures in the most vulnerable communities and systems in the world.

Adaptation is essential to address the impacts resulting from the warming which is already unavoidable due to past emissions. But, adaptation alone is not expected to cope with all the projected effects of climate change, and especially not in the long run as most impacts increase in magnitude.

There is substantial potential for the mitigation of global greenhouse gas emissions over the coming decades that could offset the projected growth of global emissions or reduce emissions below current levels. There are multiple drivers for actions that reduce emissions of greenhouse gases, and they can produce multiple benefits at the local level in terms of economic development and poverty alleviation, employment, energy security, and local environmental protection.

The Fourth Assessment Report has assessed the costs of mitigation in the coming decades for a number of scenarios of stabilisation of the concentration of these gases and associated average global temperature increases at equilibrium. A stabilisation level of 445–590 ppm [parts per million] of CO_2 [carbon dioxide] equivalent, which corresponds to a global average temperature increase above pre-industrial at equilibrium (using best estimate climate sensitivity) of around 2.0–2.4°C would lead to a reduction in average annual GDP [gross domestic product] growth rate of less than 0.12% up to 2030 and beyond up to 2050. Essentially, the range of global GDP reduction with the least-cost trajectory assessed for this level of stabilisation would be less than 3% in 2030 and less than 5.5% in 2050. Some important characteristics of this stabilisation scenario need careful consideration:

- For a CO_2-equivalent concentration at stabilization of 445–490 ppm, CO_2 emissions would need to peak during the period 2000–15 and decline thereafter. We, therefore, have a short window of time to bring about a reduction in global emissions if we wish to limit temperature increase to around 2°C at equilibrium

- Even with this ambitious level of stabilisation the global average sea level rise above pre-industrial at equilibrium from thermal expansion only would lie between 0.4–1.4 metres. This would have serious implications for several regions and locations in the world

A rational approach to management of risk would require that human society evaluates the impacts of climate change inherent in a business-as-usual scenario and the quantifiable costs as well as unquantifiable damages associated with it, against the cost of action. With such an approach, the overwhelming result would be in favour of major efforts at mitigation. The impacts of climate change even with current levels of concentration of greenhouse gases would be serious enough to justify stringent mitigation efforts. If the concentration of all greenhouse gases and aerosols had been kept constant at year 2000 levels, a further warming of about 0.1°C per decade would be expected. Subsequent temperature projections depend on specific emission scenarios. Those systems and communities, which are vulnerable, may suffer considerably with even small changes in the climate at the margin.

Science tells us not only that the climate system is changing, but also that further warming and sea level rise is in store even if greenhouse gases were to be stabilized today. That is a consequence of the basic physics of the system. Social factors also contribute to our future, including the 'lock-in' due, for example, to today's power plants, transportation systems, and buildings, and their likely continuing emissions even as cleaner future infrastructure comes on line. So the challenge before us is not only a large one, it is also one in which every year of delay implies a commitment to greater climate change in the future.

It would be relevant to recall the words of President Gayoom of the Maldives at the Forty Second Session of the UN General Assembly on the 19 October 1987:

> "As for my own country, the Maldives, a mean sea level rise of 2 metres would suffice to virtually submerge the entire country of 1,190 small islands, most of which barely rise 2 metres above mean sea level. That would be the death of a nation. With a mere 1 metre rise also, a storm surge would be catastrophic, and possibly fatal to the nation."

On 22 September 1997, at the opening of the thirteenth session of the IPCC at Male, the capital of the Maldives, President Gayoom reminded us of the threat to his country when he said, "Ten years ago, in April 1987, this very spot where we are gathered now, was under two feet of water, as unusually high waves inundated one third of Male, as well as the Male International Airport and several other islands of our archipelago." Hazards from the impacts of climate change are, therefore, a reality today in some parts of the world, and we cannot hide under global averages and the ability of affluent societies to deal with climate-related threats as opposed to the condition of vulnerable communities in poor regions of the globe.

The successive assessment reports published by the IPCC since 1990 demonstrate the progress of scientific knowledge about climate change and its consequences. This progress has been made possible by the combined strength of growing evidence of the observations of changes in climate, dedicated work from the scientific community, and improved efforts in communication of science. We have now more scientific evidence of the reality of climate change and its human contribution. As stated in the Fourth Assessment Report, "warming of the climate system is unequivocal", and "most of the global average warming over the past 50 years is very likely due to anthropogenic greenhouse gases increases".

What Needs to Be Done in Order to Combat Climate Change

Further progress in scientific assessment needs however to be achieved in order to support strong and adequate responses to the threats of climate change, including adaptation and mitigation policies.

There is also notable lack of geographic data and literature on observed changes, with marked scarcity in developing countries. Future changes in the Greenland and Antarctic ice sheet mass are another major source of uncertainty that could increase sea level rise projections. The need for further scientific input calls for continued trust and cooperation from policy makers and society at large to support the work needed for scientific progress.

How climate change will affect peace is for others to determine, but we have provided scientific assessment of what could become a basis for conflict. When Mr Willy Brandt spoke at the acceptance of the Nobel Peace Prize in 1971, he said, ". . . we shall have to know more about the origins of conflicts. . . . As I see it, next to reasonable politics, learning is in our world the true credible alternative to force." . . .

The work of the IPCC has helped the world to learn more on all aspects of climate change, and the Nobel Peace Prize Committee has acknowledged this fact. The question is whether [governments] will support what Willy Brandt referred to as "reasonable politics". Will those responsible for decisions in the field of climate change at the global level listen to the voice of science and knowledge, which is now loud and clear? If they do so . . . then all my colleagues in the IPCC and those thousands toiling for the cause of science would feel doubly honoured at the privilege I am receiving today on their behalf.

World's Scientists Acknowledge Uncertainties and Disagreements, but Most Agree Climate Change Is a Real Threat

Fred Pearce

Fred Pearce, reporting for New Scientist, *notes that while there is a scientific consensus that anthropogenic, or human-driven, climate change is happening, there are healthy disagreements about how it happens and its likely effects. Pearce talks with scientists about these points of disagreement, their significance, and their effect on the public understanding of climate change. Pearce is an environmental writer and frequent contributor to* New Scientist, *a science and technology magazine and news service.*

As you read, consider the following questions:

1. The Mauna Loa observatory in Hawaii has been charting global warming for sixty years. According to Mauna Loa, how much has the earth's temperature increased since pre-industrialization?

2. What types of greenhouse gas emissions are making atmosphere temperatures warmer?

3. How does the melting of polar ice amplify global warming?

On 16 February [2005], the Kyoto Protocol [an international agreement to reduce greenhouse gases] comes into force. Whether you see this as a triumph of international cooperation or a case of too little, too late, there is no doubt that it was only made possible by decades of dedicated work by climate scientists. Yet as these same researchers celebrate their most notable achievement, their work is being denigrated as never before.

The hostile criticism is coming from sceptics [skeptics] who question the reality of climate change. Critics have always been around, but in recent months their voices have become increasingly prominent and influential. One British newspaper called climate change a "global fraud" based on "left-wing, anti-American, anti-west ideology". A London-based think tank described the UK's [United Kingdom's] chief scientific adviser, David King, as "an embarrassment" for believing that climate change is a bigger threat than terrorism. And the best-selling author Michael Crichton, in his much publicised new novel *State of Fear*, portrays global warming as an evil plot perpetrated by environmental extremists.

The winning side in the climate debate will shape economic, political, and technological developments for years, even centuries, to come.

If the sceptics are to be believed, the evidence for global warming is full of holes and the field is riven with argument and uncertainty. The apparent scientific consensus over global warming only exists, they say, because it is enforced by a scientific establishment riding the gravy train, aided and abetted by governments keen to play the politics of fear. It's easy to dismiss such claims as politically motivated and with no basis in fact—especially as the majority of sceptics are economists, business people or politicians, not scientists. But there are nagging doubts. Could the sceptics be onto something? Are we, after all, being taken for a ride?

This is perhaps the most crucial scientific question of the 21st century. The winning side in the climate debate will shape economic, political, and technological developments for years, even centuries, to come. With so much at stake, it is crucial that the right side wins. But which side is right? What is the evidence that human activity is warming the world and how reliable is it?

Is Human Activity Warming the World?

First, the basic physics. It is beyond doubt that certain gases in the atmosphere, most importantly water vapour and carbon dioxide, trap infrared radiation emitted by the earth's surface and so have a greenhouse effect. This in itself is no bad thing. Indeed, without them the planet would freeze. There is also no doubt that human activity is pumping CO_2 [carbon dioxide] into the atmosphere, and that this has caused a sustained year-on-year rise in CO_2 concentrations. For almost 60 years, measurements at the Mauna Loa observatory in Hawaii have charted this rise, and it is largely uncontested that today's concentrations are about 35 per cent above pre-industrial levels.

Temperature records from around the world going back 150 years suggest that 19 of the 20 warmest years . . . have occurred since 1980. . . .

The effect this has on the planet is also measurable. In 2000, researchers based at Imperial College London examined satellite data covering almost three decades to plot changes in the amount of infrared radiation escaping from the atmosphere into space—an indirect measure of how much heat is being trapped. In the part of the infrared spectrum trapped by CO_2—wavelengths between 13 and 19 micrometres—they found that between 1970 and 1997 less and less radiation was escaping. They concluded that the increasing quantity of atmospheric CO_2 was trapping energy that used to escape, and storing it in the atmosphere as heat. The results for the other greenhouse gases were similar.

These uncontested facts are enough to establish that "anthropogenic" [caused by humans] greenhouse gas emissions are tending to make the atmosphere warmer. What's more, there is little doubt that the climate is changing right now. Temperature records from around the world going back 150 years suggest that 19 of the 20 warmest years—measured in terms of average global temperature, which takes account of all available thermometer data—have occurred since 1980, and that four of these occurred in the past seven years.

The only serious question mark over this record is the possibility that measurements have been biased by the growth of cities near the sites where temperatures are measured, as cities retain more heat than rural areas. But some new research suggests there is no such bias. David Parker of the UK's Met Office divided the historical temperature data into two sets: one taken in calm weather and the other in windy weather. He reasoned that any effect due to nearby cities would be more pronounced in calm conditions, when the wind could not disperse the heat. There was no difference.

It is at this point, however, that uncertainty starts to creep in. Take the grand claim made by some climate researchers that the 1990s were the warmest decade in the warmest century of the past millennium. This claim is embodied in the famous "hockey stick" curve, produced by Michael Mann of the University of Virginia in 1998, based on "proxy" records of past temperature, such as air bubbles in ice cores and growth rings in tree and coral. Sceptics have attacked the findings over poor methodology used, and their criticism has been confirmed by climate modellers, who have recently recognised that such proxy studies systematically underestimate past variability. As one Met Office scientist put it: "We cannot make claims as to the 1990s being the warmest decade."

There is also room for uncertainty in inferences drawn from the rise in temperature over the past 150 years. The warming itself is real enough, but that doesn't necessarily mean that human activity is to blame. Sceptics say that the warming could be natural, and again they have a point. It is now recognised that up to 40 per cent of the climatic variation since 1890 is probably due to two natural phenomena. The first is solar cycles, which influence the amount of radiation reaching the earth, and some scientist have argued that increased solar activity can account for most of the warming of the past 150 years. The second is the changing frequency of volcanic eruptions, which produce airborne particles that can shade and hence cool the planet for a year or more. This does not mean, however, that the sceptics can claim victory, as no known natural effects can explain the 0.5°C warming seen in the past 30 years. In fact, natural changes alone would have caused a marginal global cooling.

How Hot Will it Get?

In the face of such evidence, the vast majority of scientists, even sceptical ones, now agree that our activities are making the planet warmer, and that we can expect more warming as we release more CO_2 into the atmosphere. This leaves two critical questions. How much warming can we expect? And how much should we care about it? Here the uncertainties begin in earnest.

The concentration of CO_2 in the atmosphere now stands at around 375 parts per million. A doubling of CO_2 from pre-industrial levels of 280 parts per million, which could happen as early as 2050, will add only about 1°C to average global temperatures, other things being equal. But if there's one thing we can count on, it is that other things will not be equal; some important things will change.

All experts agree that the planet is likely to respond in a variety of ways, some of which will dampen down the warming (negative feedback) while others will amplify it (positive feedback). Assessing the impacts of these feedbacks has been a central task of the UN's [United Nations] Intergovernmental Panel on Climate Change, a cooperative agency set up 17 years ago that has harnessed the work of thousands of scientists. Having spent countless hours of supercomputer time creating and refining models to simulate the planet's climate system, the IPCC concludes that the feedbacks will be overwhelmingly positive. The only question, it says, is just how big this positive feedback will be.

The latest IPCC assessment is that doubling CO_2 levels will warm the world by anything from 1.4 to 5.8°C. In other words, this predicts a rise in global temperature from pre-industrial levels of around 14.8°C to between 16.2 and 20.6°C. Even at the low end, this is probably the biggest fluctuation in temperature that has occurred in the history of human civilisation. But uncertainties within the IPCC models remain, and the sceptics charge that they are so great that this conclusion is not worth the paper it is written on. So what are the positive feedbacks and how much uncertainty surrounds them?

Melting of polar ice is almost certainly one. Where the ice melts, the new, darker surface absorbs more heat from the sun, and so warms the planet. This is already happening. The second major source of positive feedback is water vapour. As this is responsible for a bigger slice of today's greenhouse effect than any other gas, including CO_2, any change in the amount of moisture in the atmosphere is critical. A warmer world will evaporate more water from the oceans, giving an extra push to warming. But there is a complication. Some of the water vapour will turn to cloud, and the net effect of cloudier skies on heat coming in and going out is far from clear. Clouds reflect energy from the sun back into space, but they also trap heat radiated from the surface, especially at night. Whether warming or cooling predominates depends on the type and height of clouds. The IPCC calculates that the combined effect of extra water vapour and clouds will increase warming, but accepts that clouds are the biggest source of uncertainty in the models.

Sceptics who pounce on such uncertainties should remember, however, that they cut both ways. Indeed, new research based on thousands of different climate simulation models run using the spare computing capacity of idling PCs, suggest that doubling CO_2 levels could increase temperatures by as much as 11°C.

Recent analysis suggests that clouds could have a more powerful warming effect than once thought—possibly much more powerful. And there could be other surprise positive feedbacks that do not yet feature in the climate models. For instance, a release of some of the huge quantities of methane, a potent greenhouse gas, that are frozen into the Siberian permafrost and the ocean floor could have a catastrophic warming effect. And an end to ice formation in the Arctic could upset ocean currents and even shut down the Gulf Stream—the starting point for the blockbuster movie *The Day After Tomorrow*.

There are counterbalancing negative feedbacks, some of which are already in the models. These include the ability of the oceans to absorb heat from the atmosphere, and of some pollutants—such as the sulphate particles that make acid rain—to shade the planet. But both are double-edged. The models predict that the ocean's ability to absorb heat will decline as the surface warms, as mixing between less dense, warm surface waters and the denser cold depths becomes more difficult. Meanwhile, sulphate and other aerosols could already be masking far stronger underlying warming effects than are apparent from measured temperatures. Aerosols last only a few weeks in the atmosphere, while greenhouse gases last for decades. So efforts to cut pollution by using technolo-

Climate Cycle Shows Periods of Cooling and Warming

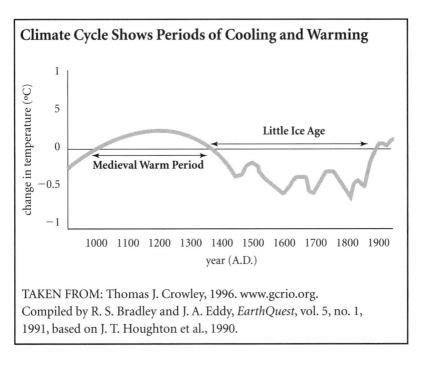

TAKEN FROM: Thomas J. Crowley, 1996. www.gcrio.org.
Compiled by R. S. Bradley and J. A. Eddy, *EarthQuest*, vol. 5, no. 1,
1991, based on J. T. Houghton et al., 1990.

gies such as scrubbers to remove sulphur dioxide from power station stacks could trigger a surge in temperatures.

Sceptics also like to point out that most models do not yet include negative feedback from vegetation, which is already growing faster in a warmer world, and soaking up more CO_2. But here they may be onto a loser, as the few climate models so far to include plants show that continued climate change is likely to damage their ability to absorb CO_2, potentially turning a negative feedback into a positive one.

Achilles' Heel?

More credible is the suggestion that some other important negative feedbacks have been left out. One prominent sceptic, meteorologist Richard Lindzen of the Massachusetts Institute of Technology, has made an interesting case that warming may dry out the upper levels of the innermost atmospheric layer, the troposphere, and less water means a weaker greenhouse effect. Lindzen, who is one of the few sceptics with a research back record that most climate scientists respect, says this dying effect could negate all the positive feedbacks and bring the warming effect of a doubling of CO_2 levels back to 1°C. While there is little data to back up his idea, some studies suggest that these outer reaches are not as warm as IPCC models predict. This could be a mere wrinkle in the models or something more important. But if catastrophists have an Achilles' heel, this could be it.

Where does this leave us? Actually, with a surprising degree of consensus about the basic science of global warming—at least among scientists. As science historian Naomi Oreskes of the University of California, San Diego, wrote in *Science* late last year: "Politicians, economists, journalists and others may have the impression of confusion, disagreement or discord among climate scientists, but that impression is incorrect."

Her review of all 928 peer-reviewed papers on climate change published between 1993 and 2003 showed the consensus to be real and near universal. Even sceptical scientists now accept that we can expect some warming. They differ from the rest only in that they believe most climate models overestimate the positive feedback and underestimate the negative, and they predict that warming will be at the bottom end of the IPCC's scale.

For the true hard-liners, of course, the scientific consensus must, by definition, be wrong. As far as they are concerned, the thousands of scientists behind the IPCC models have either been seduced by their own doom-laden narrative or are engaged in a gigantic conspiracy. They say we are faced with what the philosopher of science Thomas Kuhn called a "paradigm problem".

"Most scientists spend their lives working to shore up the reigning world view—the dominant paradigm—and those who disagree are always much fewer in number," says climatologist Patrick Michaels of the University of Virginia in Charlottesville, a leading proponent of this view. The drive to conformity is accentuated by peer review, which ensures that only papers in support of the paradigm appear in the literature, Michaels says, and by public funding that gives money to research into the prevailing "paradigm of doom". Rebels who challenge prevailing orthodoxies are often proved right, he adds.

But even if you accept this sceptical view of how science is done, it doesn't mean the orthodoxy is always wrong. We know for sure that human activity is influencing the global environment, even if we don't know by how much. We might still get away with it: the sceptics could be right and the majority of the world's climate scientists wrong. It would be a lucky break. But how lucky do you feel?

Climate Change Skeptics Do Not Receive Equal Funding

Jeff Mason

Some researchers claim that the international scientific community discourages open discussion on climate change. The researchers, many of whom disagree with some aspect of the current scientific consensus on climate change, assert that they have trouble getting their work published and obtaining research funding. Furthermore, they claim that too many national governments are basing their climate change policy solely on the findings of the United Nations Intergovernmental Panel on Climate Change (IPCC) without considering other research. Jeff Mason is a staff reporter for Reuters, an international newswire service.

As you read, consider the following questions:

1. European Union officials are attempting to cut greenhouse gas emissions in 2020 by how much?
2. What group is considered the "world authority" on the issue of global warming?
3. Which British economist feels that governments have given the Intergovernmental Panel on Climate Change a monopoly on climate advice?

Skeptics of the seriousness of global warming complained on Wednesday [April 2007] of not being heard by the public or policy makers while warning governments to take a second look at the scientific consensus on climate change.

Scientists who doubt the scope and cause of climate change have trouble getting funding and academic posts unless they conform to an "alarmist scenario," said Roger Helmer, a British member of the European Parliament, at a panel discussion on appropriate responses to rising global temperatures.

"If global warming is happening, we can then ask: is it accelerating and is it likely to be catastrophic?" he said. "Many people think not."

European Union [EU] leaders agreed in March [2007] to try to cut greenhouse gas emissions by at least a fifth compared with 1990 levels by 2020 and as much as 30 percent if other industrialized and emerging countries joined in.

Scientific journals refused to take papers from scientists who doubted climate change.

The EU pledge came shortly before the Intergovernmental Panel on Climate Change (IPCC), which groups 2,500 scientists and is considered the world authority on the issue, said all regions of the planet would suffer from a sharp warming.

David Henderson, an economist at the Westminster Business School in London and former head of the Economics and Statistics Department at the Organization for Economic Cooperation and Development, the OECD, said governments had given the IPCC a monopoly on climate advice.

"The very idea of creating a single would-be authoritative fount of wisdom is itself dubious," he said, urging countries to seek a more balanced approach than the IPCC and to stop pursuing programs to urgently reduce carbon emissions.

"In this area of policy it's high time for governments to think again," he said.

ExxonMobil Cuts Back Its Funding for Climate Skeptics

ExxonMobil, the world's largest publicly traded company, recently said it would stop funding a number of groups that are skeptical of climate change. But this is not the first time ExxonMobil has made such a commitment, prompting questions about its sincerity. The company's critics have long accused it of sponsoring a disinformation campaign that portrayed climate scientists as much more divided about global warming than they really are.

According to a 2007 report by the Union of Concerned Scientists, between 1998 and 2005, Exxon gave $16 million [U.S. dollars] to organizations skeptical of climate change. Exxon also headed a task force whose goal was to manufacture doubt about global warming.

Monica Heger,
"ExxonMobil Cuts Back Its Funding for Climate Skeptics,"
July 2008. www.spectrum.ieee.org.

Mahi Sideridou, climate policy director at environmental group Greenpeace, rejected criticism of the IPCC.

"Saying that the IPCC is not balanced is probably the most ridiculous claim that anybody can make," she said, stressing the group's reports were based on scientific consensus.

The IPCC findings are approved unanimously by more than 100 governments and will guide policy on issues such as extending the U.N.'s [United Nations'] Kyoto Protocol, the main U.N. plan for capping greenhouse gas emissions, beyond 2012.

Benny Peiser, a professor at Liverpool John Moores University, questioned the methods used by climate scientists. He said many were recognizing that using computer modeling to predict an "inherently unpredictable future" was illogical.

"Today's scientific consensus very often turns out to be tomorrow's redundant theory," he said. He said that scientific journals refused to take papers from scientists who doubted climate change.

Most scientists say climate change will cause seas to rise, glaciers to melt and storms to intensify, potentially leading to more natural disasters around the world.

European Union Nations Assert That Policies of the United States Fail to Address Climate Change

Markus Becker and Holger Dambeck

Markus Becker and Holger Dambeck report on international opinions of the United States's hesitation to join international emissions agreements during the early days of the December 2007 United Nations climate change conference in Bali, Indonesia. The authors assert that the member nations of the European Union are increasingly frustrated by a perceived lack of action and cooperation from the United States on climate change issues. In the final hours of the conference, the United States delegation reversed its position and agreed to further negotiations on emissions reduction targets. Reporters Markus Becker and Holger Dambeck covered the Bali Conference for the German-based magazine Der Spiegel.

As you read, consider the following questions:

1. The goal of the Bali meeting was to find an international climate change agreement to replace what soon-to-expire agreement?
2. What two countries are the most responsible for greenhouse gas emissions?

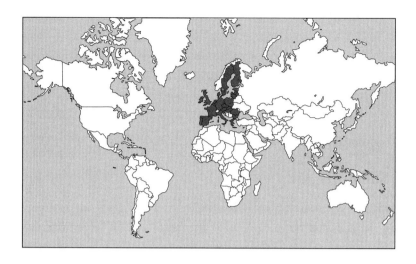

3. What political party released a report accusing the White House of manipulating climate change science?

When it comes to climate change, America's image in the world is hardly the best. Wherever countries are trying to limit emissions of greenhouse gases, the [United States] US—and especially the administration of President George W. Bush—is seen as a dangerous spoilsport, doing what it can to torpedo far-reaching climate agreements.

It is a role, recent US statements lead one to hope, the country may be tired of playing. The climate change conference . . . held on the Indonesian island of Bali [in 2007] is the beginning of a process to find an international climate change agreement to succeed the soon-to-expire Kyoto Protocol. American diplomats there have been doing their best to sound as though the US wants to be part of the solution.

"The IPCC has made it clear that climate change is a serious challenge," Paula Dobriansky, US undersecretary of state for democracy and global affairs and head of the US delegation at Bali, told reporters on Wednesday [December 2007]. "We have to respond to that challenge and open a new chapter of climate diplomacy." She wants that chapter to be opened right away, she said.

Dobriansky wasn't finished. She said it was vital for the international community to come up with a "roadmap" for negotiations, eventually leading to a climate treaty ready for signing at the 2009 climate summit in Copenhagen [capital of Denmark]. The new agreement, she continued, should be both environmentally and economically effective. "We want the world's largest economies, including the United States, to be part of the global arrangement," she said.

The US position ... continues to be that of an impassable barricade on the road to an international strategy to tackle climate change.

"National Commitments"

Not to be outdone, James Connaughton, senior environmental advisor to President Bush, insists that the US wants "national commitments" for those countries responsible for the most greenhouse gas emissions. The US is on top of that list, with China coming in a close second.

But for all the talk, the US position at Bali continues to be that of an impassable barricade on the road to an international strategy to tackle climate change. "National commitments," as the US insists, should remain voluntary, and the negotiators from America have continuously rejected any verbiage that even hints at mandatory climate reduction goals, as the European Union [EU] wants.

Indeed, United Nations Secretary-General Ban Ki-moon on Wednesday said that specific guidelines on emissions cuts might have to wait for subsequent negotiating sessions. "Realistically, it may be too ambitious," to try and impose concrete emissions reduction goals now. "Practically speaking, this will have to be negotiated down the road."

Just what those negotiations might look like is difficult to say. The EU continues to insist on stringent targets necessary,

EU negotiators say, to avoid a more than 2 degree Celsius (3.6 degree Fahrenheit) rise in the earth's average temperature, relative to pre-industrial levels. Bush prefers that industry commit itself to voluntary goals.

"I Hope That Will Change"

Former US Vice President Al Gore, who was awarded the Nobel Peace Prize [2007] last weekend for his work on climate change, accused his country of trying to block a climate agreement. "The position of the administration in the US right now appears to be to try to block any progress in Bali. I hope that will change," Gore said.

Indeed, there are few who still believe that the Bali conference will result in a commitment to concrete emissions reductions. Even the term "binding targets" has become a no-no among those directing the negotiations. In deference to the US position, the term "quantifiable targets" is now being favored. But Washington has indicated its discomfort even with that formulation. Numbers, the US negotiating team has made clear, are an anathema; head US negotiator Harlan Watson said: "Once numbers appear in the text, it predetermines outcomes and it can really drive negotiations in one direction."

Should one want a slightly clearer enunciation of what, exactly, the Bush administration's position is on global warming, one only has to look across the Pacific Ocean to San Francisco. There, the American Geophyisical Union is meeting this week, and the 15,000 scientists gathered there are discussing climate change. On Monday, John Marburger, chief science advisor to the American president, spoke to the conference, in a talk entitled "Reflections on the Science and Policy of Energy and Climate Change."

"It is difficult these days to speak reasonably about climate change," he said. It doesn't make any sense, he went on, to force growing economies like those of China or India to accept emissions limits. "They want to improve their lives," he said. He also explained why the US couldn't drastically reduce its CO_2 [carbon dioxide] emissions: "The costs are very high. We can't just ignore economic competition."

"Too Ambitious"

Ban Ki-moon, it would seem from his comments on Wednesday, has been listening. He said that Bali would be considered a success if a time line for subsequent negotiations—with the goal of an agreement by 2009—could be agreed upon. But he also issued a clear warning: "We are at a crossroad," he said to the delegates from over 180 nations. "One path leads to a comprehensive climate change agreement, the other to oblivion. The choice is clear." He also, though, said that the European goal of binding rich nations to cut emissions by 25 to 40 percent relative to 1990 levels was "too ambitious."

German Environment Minister Sigmar Gabriel, at the Bali conference since Tuesday, likewise said that the goal of this month's conference is not the formulation of concrete goals. There will, after all, be subsequent negotiations. But, he said, it is also unacceptable to end the conference with no agreements at all. "I don't need a paper from Bali that says we will just meet again next year," he said. "If you want to go a long way, you need to know the starting point and where you want to go."

It continues to look as though the White House would have to make a 180 degree change of course.

In order to help find that starting point, the Indonesian hosts of the conference have suggested bringing together a smaller group of ministers to negotiate the fine points. Five members will be representing the EU in the smaller assembly: Gabriel from Germany, his counterparts from Portugal (as current holder of the rotating EU presidency) and Slovenia (as

Not the End of the World As We Know It

Svante Arrhenius, the father of the greenhouse effect, would be called a heretic today. Far from issuing the sort of dire predictions about climate change which are common nowadays, the Swedish physicist dared to predict a paradise on Earth for humans when he announced, in April 1896, that temperatures were rising—and that it would be a blessing for all.

Arrhenius, who later won the Nobel Prize in Chemistry, calculated that the release of carbon dioxide—or carbonic acid as it was then known—through burning coal, oil and natural gas would lead to a significant rise in temperatures worldwide. But, he argued, "by the influence of the increasing percentage of carbonic acid in the atmosphere, we may hope to enjoy ages with more equable and better climates," potentially making poor harvests and famine a thing of the past.

Arrhenius was merely expressing a view that was firmly entrenched in the collective consciousness of the day: warm times are good times; cold times are bad. . . .

But how bad is climate change really? Will global warming trigger plagues of Biblical proportions? Can we look forward to endless droughts and catastrophic floods?

Or will Arrhenius end up being right after all? Could rising temperatures lead to higher crop yields and more tourism in many places? In other words, is humanity actually creating new paradises?

The truth is probably somewhere between these two extremes. Climate change will undoubtedly have losers—but it will also have winners. There will be a reshuffling of climate zones on earth. And there is something else that we can already say with certainty: The end of the world isn't coming any time soon.

Olaf Stampf, "Not the End of the World As We Know It,"
Der Spiegel Online, *May 7, 2007.*

the next EU president), the EU Commission and, as host of the Copenhagen Conference in 2009, Denmark.

Whether this move will ultimately succeed in getting the US along with China and India—as the most important developing countries—remains to be seen. As does an indication as to how committed the US is to its rhetoric of wanting to be part of a climate agreement. For the moment, however, it continues to look as though the White House would have to make a 180 degree change of course. This Wednesday, Democrats in Congress released a report accusing the White House of having manipulated climate science for years.

"The Bush administration has engaged in a systematic effort to manipulate climate change science and mislead policy makers and the public about the dangers of global warming," the report, from the House Committee on Oversight and Government Reform, said James Connaughton was fingered as one of those responsible.

United Kingdom Research Group Asserts That Climate Change May Benefit Humans

Antony Barnett and Mark Townsend

Antony Barnett and Mark Townsend report for the United Kingdom-based newspaper, The Observer, *on the emergence of a British think tank skeptical of mainstream climate change claims. The organization's first report states that climate change could benefit certain groups of people, claiming that the rise in sea levels will be miniscule and that warm weather may boost agriculture in some regions. Barnett and Townsend, as well as spokespersons from environmental groups, note that the organization's statements differ from the scientific consensus and assert that they are politically motivated.*

As you read, consider the following questions:

1. The International Policy Network believes the rise in sea level will reach a maximum of what?

2. According to the International Policy Network, what really causes "extreme weather?"

3. How does the International Policy Network believe global warming could benefit mankind?

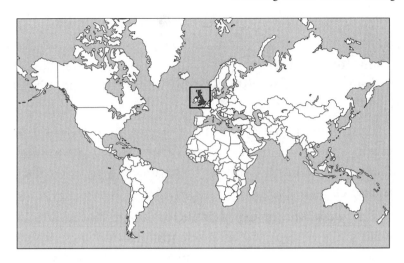

Climate change is 'a myth', sea levels are not rising and Britain's chief scientist is 'an embarrassment' for believing catastrophe is inevitable. These are the controversial views of a new London-based think tank that will publish a report tomorrow [November 2004] attacking the apocalyptic view that man-made greenhouse gases will destroy the planet.

The International Policy Network will publish its long-awaited study, claiming that the science warning of an environmental disaster caused by climate change is 'fatally flawed'. It will state that previous predictions of changes in sea level of a metre over the next 100 years were overestimates.

Controversial Claims

Instead, the report will say that sea level rises will reach a maximum of just 20 cms during the next century, adding that global warming could, in fact, benefit mankind by increasing fish stocks.

The report's views closely mirror those held by many of President George Bush's senior advisers, who have been accused of derailing attempts to reach international agreement over how to prevent climate change.

The report is set to cause controversy. The network . . . has received cash donations from the US [United States] oil giant ExxonMobil, which has long lobbied against the climate change agenda. Exxon lists the donation as part of its 'climate change outreach' programme.

Environmentalists yesterday [November 2004] said the network report was an attempt by American neo-conservatives to sabotage the Prime Minister's attempts to lead the world in tackling climate change.

Last week, the network's director Julian Morris attacked Britain's highly respected chief scientist. 'David King is an embarrassment to himself and an embarrassment to his country.' He criticised preparations by Tony Blair [British Prime Minister] to use his presidency of the world's most powerful nations next year to lead attempts in tackling climate change.

Morris described Blair's plans to use his G8 [Group of Eight, an international forum of developed countries] tenure to halt global warming as 'offensive'. Bush is understood to have objected to Blair placing the issue at the top of the agenda and to the robust tone of his recent speeches on climate change.

Tomorrow's findings echo a number of [statistician Bjorn] Lomborg's themes, as well as maintaining that 'extreme weather' is more likely caused by a natural cycle rather than man-made.

Public Does Not Share Passion for Reducing Greenhouse Gases

Blair, however, has garnered considerable international support for describing the issue as 'the single, biggest long-term issue' facing the world. According to the network, however, his passion on the matter is not shared by the British public. A

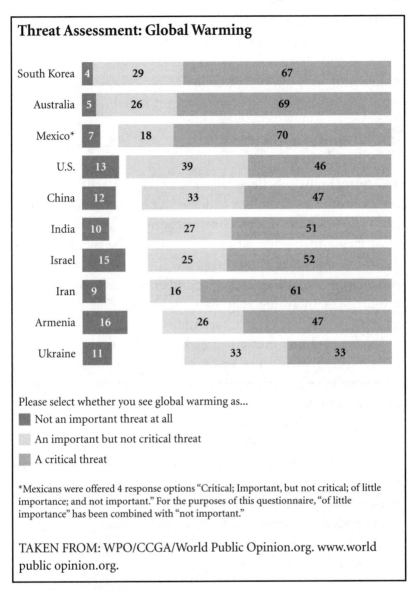

Threat Assessment: Global Warming

Please select whether you see global warming as...
- Not an important threat at all
- An important but not critical threat
- A critical threat

*Mexicans were offered 4 response options "Critical; Important, but not critical; of little importance; and not important." For the purposes of this questionnaire, "of little importance" has been combined with "not important."

TAKEN FROM: WPO/CCGA/World Public Opinion.org. www.world public opinion.org.

poll it commissioned claims six out of 10 Britons believe Blair should not implement the Kyoto Protocol if it will harm the economy.

The executive director of the environment group Greenpeace, Stephen Tindale, said: 'We've been watching how the network employs the same tactics as Washington neo-cons. . . .

'For years, the tobacco companies blocked action on smoking by sowing doubt about the science. Esso [ExxonMobil] and its friends have done the same thing in the US on climate change and now they're busy in Britain. Global warming is the biggest threat we face, the science is certain.'

Challenging the Science of Climate Change

Environmentalists believe this week's report will provoke a similar storm to that inspired by Danish statistician Bjorn Lomborg, who maintains climate change is not the greatest threat facing mankind and resources should be spent on more pressing issues, such as tackling HIV.

Tomorrow's findings echo a number of Lomborg's themes, as well as maintaining that 'extreme weather' is more likely caused by a natural cycle rather than man-made. It also challenges assumptions that climate change will lead to a rise in malaria along with more positive effects, such as increasing fish stocks in the north Atlantic and reducing the incidence of temperature-related deaths among vulnerable people.

Morris admitted receiving money from a number of companies, including $50,000 from Exxon, but denied the organisation was a front for neo-conservative opinion. 'I have written about these issues for many years. If a company wants to provide money, then I'd be happy to accept it.'

He added that his $1 million budget is small compared to those of international groups, such as Greenpeace and Friends of the Earth.

United States Congress Alleges Federal Interference with Climate Change Science

United States House of Representatives, Committee on Oversight and Government Reform

In 2006, the United States Congress began an investigation of over 27,000 pages of documents relating to White House executive policy on climate change under the administration of President George W. Bush. The investigating committee concluded that the White House censored government scientists, restricted their ability to report their findings in the media, and systematically edited documents that mentioned certain aspects of climate change. This report was produced as a result of an inquiry by the United States Congress.

As you read, consider the following questions:

1. Dr. Thomas Karl, director of the National Climatic Data Center, had his testimony heavily edited by the White House. What became of his comment that global warming "is playing" a role in increased hurricane intensity?
2. How many edits were made to the administration's *Strategic Plan of the Climate Change Science Program?*
3. What Supreme Court case rejected the final opinion incorporating White House edits?

United States House of Representatives, Committee on Oversight and Government Reform, "Executive Summary," *Political Interference with Climate Change Science Under the Bush Administration*, December 12, 2007. http://oversight.house.gov.

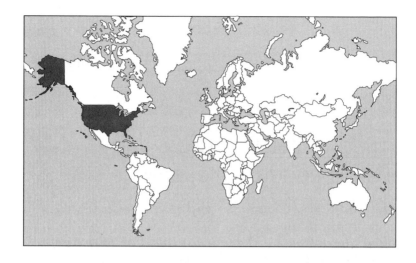

For the past sixteen months, the House Oversight and Government Reform Committee has been investigating allegations of political interference with government climate change science under the [George W.] Bush administration. During the course of this investigation, the Committee obtained over 27,000 pages of documents from the White House Council on Environmental Quality (CEQ) and the Commerce Department, held two investigative hearings, and deposed or interviewed key officials. Much of the information made available to the Committee has never been publicly disclosed.

This report presents the findings of the Committee's investigation. The evidence before the Committee leads to one inescapable conclusion: The Bush administration has engaged in a systematic effort to manipulate climate change science and mislead policy makers and the public about the dangers of global warming.

In 1998, the American Petroleum Institute developed an internal "Communications Action Plan" that stated: "Victory will be achieved when ... average citizens 'understand' uncertainties in climate science ... [and] recognition of uncertainties becomes part of the 'conventional wisdom.'" The Bush administration has acted as if the oil industry's communications

plan were its mission statement. White House officials and political appointees in the agencies censored congressional testimony on the causes and impacts of global warming, con-
trolled media access to government climate scientists, and
edited federal scientific reports to inject unwarranted uncertainty into discussions of climate change and to minimize the
threat to the environment and the economy.

The White House Censored Climate Change Scientists

The White House exerted unusual control over the public
statements of federal scientists on climate change issues. It was
standard practice for media requests to speak with federal scientists on climate change matters to be sent to CEQ for White
House approval. By controlling which government scientists
could respond to media inquiries, the White House suppressed
dissemination of scientific views that could conflict with administration policies. The White House also edited congressional testimony regarding the science of climate change.

---

*In the case of EPA's [Environmental Protection Agency's]
Air Trends Report, CEQ went beyond editing and simply vetoed the entire climate change section of the report.*

Former CEQ Chief of Staff Philip Cooney told the Committee: "Our communications people would render a view as
to whether someone should give an interview or not and who
it should be." According to Kent Laborde, a career public affairs officer at the National Oceanic and Atmospheric Administration, media requests related to climate change issues were
handled differently from other requests because "I would have
to route media inquires through CEQ." This practice was particularly evident after Hurricane Katrina. Mr. Laborde was
asked, "Did the White House and the Department of Commerce not want scientists who believed that climate change

Inquiry Sought on Agency Memo About Polar Bears, Climate Change

Two senior House Democrats demanded ... that Interior Secretary Dirk Kempthorne turn over documents to Congress in order to determine whether the administration was preventing federal scientists traveling abroad from discussing how global warming affects polar bears. ...

The memo, which was reported in other media on Thursday [March 2007], cautioned employees against speaking about the relationship between climate change and the possible extinction of polar bears without getting official approval in advance.

Juliet Eilperin, "Inquiry Sought on Agency Memo About Polar Bears, Climate Change," Washington Post, March 10, 2007.

was increasing hurricane activity talking with the press?" He responded: "There was a consistent approach that might have indicated that."

White House officials and agency political appointees also altered congressional testimony regarding the science of climate change. The changes to the recent climate change testimony of Dr. Julie Gerberding, the Director of the Centers for Disease Control and Prevention, have received considerable attention. A year earlier, when Dr. Thomas Karl, the Director of National Climatic Data Center, appeared before the House Oversight Committee, his testimony was also heavily edited by both White House officials and political appointees at the Commerce Department. He was not allowed to say in his written testimony that "modern climate change is dominated by human influences," that "we are venturing into the unknown territory with changes in climate," or that "it is very likely (>95 percent probability) that humans are largely responsible for many of the observed changes in climate." His assertion that global warming "is playing" a role in increased hurricane intensity became "may play."

The White House Extensively Edited Climate Change Reports

There was a systematic White House effort to minimize the significance of climate change by editing climate change reports. CEQ Chief of Staff Phil Cooney and other CEQ officials made at least 294 edits to the administration's *Strategic Plan of the Climate Change Science Program* to exaggerate or emphasize scientific uncertainties or to deemphasize or diminish the importance of the human role in global warming.

The White House insisted on edits to EPA's [Environmental Protection Agency's] draft *Report on the Environment* that were so extreme that the EPA Administrator opted to eliminate the climate change section of the report. One such edit was the inclusion of a reference to a discredited, industry-funded paper. In a memo to the vice president's office, Mr. Cooney explained: "We plan to begin to refer to this study in administration communications on the science of global climate change" because it "contradicts a dogmatic view held by many in the climate science community that the past century was the warmest in the past millennium and signals of human induced 'global warming.'"

In the case of EPA's *Air Trends Report*, CEQ went beyond editing and simply vetoed the entire climate change section of the report.

Other White House Actions

The White House played a major role in crafting the August 2003 EPA legal opinion disavowing authority to regulate greenhouse gases. CEQ Chairman James Connaughton personally edited the draft legal opinion. When an EPA draft quoted the National Academy of Science conclusion that "the changes observed over the last several decades are likely mostly due to human activities," CEQ objected because "the above quotes are unnecessary and extremely harmful to the legal case being made." The first line of another internal CEQ document transmitting comments on the draft EPA legal opinion reads: "Vulnerability: science." The final opinion incorporating the White House edits was rejected by the Supreme Court in April 2007 in *Massachusetts v. EPA.*

The White House also edited a 2002 op-ed by EPA Administrator Christine Todd Whitman to ensure that it followed the White House line on climate change. Despite objections from EPA, CEQ insisted on repeating an unsupported assertion that millions of American jobs would be lost if the Kyoto Protocol were ratified.

Periodical Bibliography

The following articles have been selected to supplement the diverse views presented in this chapter.

John M. Broder — "Senate Opens Debate on Politically Risky Bill Addressing Global Warming," *The New York Times*, June 3, 2008.

Nigel Calder — "An Experiment That Hints We Are Wrong on Climate Change," February 11, 2007. www.timesonline.co.uk.

Carbon Trust — "Is Climate Change Really Happening?" 2005. www.carbontrust.co.uk.

Climate.org — "Religious Groups Becoming a Factor in Climate Policy Debate," February 24, 2006. www.climate.org.

Michael Coren — "The Science Debate Behind Climate Change," CNN, February 10, 2006. www.cnn.com.

John Donnelly — "Debate Over Global Warming Is Shifting," *The Boston Globe*, February 15, 2007.

Alister Doyle — "U.N. Climate Talks Seek Clearer Ideas," Reuters, June 12, 2008. www.reuters.com.

Juliet Eilperin — "Debate on Climate Shifts to Issue of Irreparable Change," *Washington Post*, January 29, 2006.

George C. Marshall Institute — "Climate Change," 2008. www.marshall.org.

Steven Mufson — "Climate Change Debate Hinges on Economics," *Washington Post*, July 15, 2007.

Pew Center — "The Day After Tomorrow: Could It Really Happen?" 2008. www.pewclimate.org.

Alan Wirzbicki — "Gingrich Drops Skepticism on Global Warming," *The Boston Globe*, April 11, 2007.

CHAPTER 2

The Impact of Global Climate Change

The International Economic Impacts of Climate Change: An Overview

Nicholas Stern

According to British economist Nicholas Stern, global climate change will affect basic needs for people around the world. Access to food and water, as well as a rise in climate-related disease, would cause suffering for hundreds of millions of people worldwide. Stern views curtailing greenhouse gas emissions as one solution, but notes that it requires strong policy choices by governments of both developed and developing nations.

Nicholas Stern is the former chief economist and senior vice president of World Bank from 2000 to 2003. Stern has also worked as a government economic advisor in the United Kingdom.

As you read, consider the following questions:

1. If nations do not act now to curtail global warming, the overall costs and risks of climate change will be equivalent to losing what percentage of the global gross domestic product (GDP)?

Nicholas Stern, "Summary of Conclusions," *The Stern Review Report: The Economics of Climate Change*, Cambridge, MA: Cambridge University Press, 2007, pp. vi–ix. Copyright © Cambridge University Press 2007. Reprinted with the permission of Cambridge University Press.

2. If no actions are taken to reduce emissions, the concentration of greenhouse gases in the atmosphere would commit the world to a global average temperature rise of how many degrees?

3. In what way can emissions be reduced, according to the viewpoint?

The scientific evidence is now overwhelming: climate change is a serious global threat, and it demands an urgent global response.

This [Stern] Review has assessed a wide range of evidence on the impacts of climate change and on the economic costs, and has used a number of different techniques to assess costs and risks. From all of these perspectives, the evidence gathered by the Review leads to a simple conclusion: the benefits of strong and early action far outweigh the economic costs of not acting.

Climate change will affect the basic elements of life for people around the world—access to water, food production, health, and the environment. Hundreds of millions of people could suffer hunger, water shortages, and coastal flooding as the world warms.

Using the results from formal economic models, the Review estimates that if we don't act, the overall costs and risks of climate change will be equivalent to losing at least 5% of global GDP [gross domestic product] each year, now and forever. If a wider range of risks and impacts is taken into account, the estimates of damage could rise to 20% of GDP or more.

In contrast, the costs of action—reducing greenhouse gas emissions to avoid the worst impacts of climate change—can be limited to around 1% of global GDP each year.

The investment that takes place in the next 10–20 years will have a profound effect on the climate in the second half of this century and in the next. Our actions now and over the coming decades could create risks of major disruption to economic and social activity, on a scale similar to those associated with the great wars and the economic depression of the first half of the 20th century. And it will be difficult or impossible to reverse these changes.

So prompt and strong action is clearly warranted. Because climate change is a global problem, the response to it must be international. It must be based on a shared vision of long-term goals and agreement on frameworks that will accelerate action over the next decade, and it must build on mutually reinforcing approaches at national, regional and international level.

With strong, deliberate policy choices, it is possible to reduce emissions in both developed and developing economies on the scale necessary for stabilization in the required range while continuing to grow.

Climate Change Could Have Very Serious Impacts

If no action is taken to reduce emissions, the concentration of greenhouse gases in the atmosphere could reach double its pre-industrial level as early as 2035, virtually committing us to a global average temperature rise of over 2°C. In the longer term, there would be more than a 50% chance that the temperature rise would exceed 5°C. This rise would be very dangerous indeed; it is equivalent to the change in average temperatures from the last ice age to today. Such a radical change in the physical geography of the world must lead to major changes in the human geography—where people live and how they live their lives.

Even at more moderate levels of warming, all the evidence—from detailed studies of regional and sectoral impacts of changing weather patterns through to economic models of the global effects—shows that climate change will have serious impacts on world output, on human life and on the environment.

All countries will be affected. The most vulnerable—the poorest countries and populations—will suffer earliest and most, even though they have contributed least to the causes of climate change. The costs of extreme weather, including floods, droughts and storms, are already rising, including for rich countries.

Adaptation to climate change—that is, taking steps to build resilience and minimise costs—is essential. It is no longer possible to prevent the climate change that will take place over the next two to three decades, but it is still possible to protect our societies and economies from its impacts to some extent—for example, by providing better information, improved planning and more climate-resilient crops and infrastructure. Adaptation will cost tens of billions of dollars a year in developing countries alone, and will put still further pressure on already scarce resources. Adaptation efforts, particularly in developing countries, should be accelerated.

The Costs of Stabilising the Climate Are Significant but Manageable

The risks of the worst impacts of climate change can be substantially reduced if greenhouse gas levels in the atmosphere can be stabilised between 450 and 550 ppm [parts per million] CO_2 [carbon dioxide] equivalent (CO_2e). The current level is 430 ppm CO_2e today, and it is rising at more than 2 ppm each year. Stabilisation in this range would require emissions to be at least 25% below current levels by 2050, and perhaps much more.

Ultimately, stabilisation—at whatever level—requires that annual emissions be brought down to more than 80% below current levels.

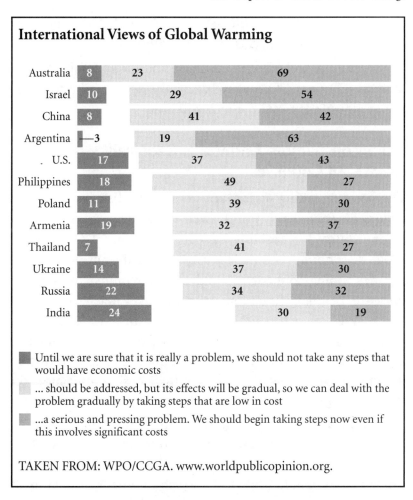

International Views of Global Warming

Australia	8	23	69
Israel	10	29	54
China	8	41	42
Argentina	—3	19	63
U.S.	17	37	43
Philippines	18	49	27
Poland	11	39	30
Armenia	19	32	37
Thailand	7	41	27
Ukraine	14	37	30
Russia	22	34	32
India	24	30	19

Until we are sure that it is really a problem, we should not take any steps that would have economic costs

... should be addressed, but its effects will be gradual, so we can deal with the problem gradually by taking steps that are low in cost

...a serious and pressing problem. We should begin taking steps now even if this involves significant costs

TAKEN FROM: WPO/CCGA. www.worldpublicopinion.org.

This is a major challenge, but sustained long-term action can achieve it at costs that are low in comparison to the risks of inaction. Central estimates of the annual costs of achieving stabilisation between 500 and 550 ppm CO_2e are around 1% of global GDP, if we start to take strong action now.

Costs could be even lower than that if there are major gains in efficiency, or if the strong co-benefits, for example from reduced air pollution, are measured. Costs will be higher if innovation in low-carbon technologies is slower than expected, or if policy makers fail to make the most of economic instruments that allow emissions to be reduced whenever, wherever and however it is cheapest to do so.

It would already be very difficult and costly to aim to stabilise at 450 ppm CO_2e. If we delay, the opportunity to stabilize at 500–550 ppm CO_2e may slip away.

Action on Climate Change Is Required Across All Countries

The costs of taking action are not evenly distributed across sectors or around the world. Even if the rich world takes on responsibility for absolute cuts in emissions of 60–80% by 2050, developing countries must take significant action too. But developing countries should not be required to bear the full costs of this action alone, and they will not have to. Carbon markets in rich countries are already beginning to deliver flows of finance to support low-carbon development, including through the Clean Development Mechanism. A transformation of these flows is now required to support action on the scale required.

Action on climate change will also create significant business opportunities, as new markets are created in low-carbon energy technologies and other low-carbon goods and services. These markets could grow to be worth hundreds of billions of dollars each year, and employment in these sectors will expand accordingly.

The world does not need to choose between averting climate change and promoting growth and development. Changes in energy technologies and in the structure of economies have created opportunities to decouple growth from greenhouse gas emissions. Indeed, ignoring climate change will eventually damage economic growth.

Tackling climate change is the pro-growth strategy for the longer term, and it can be done in a way that does not cap the aspirations for growth of rich or poor countries.

A Range of Options Exists to Cut Emissions

Emissions can be cut through increased energy efficiency, changes in demand, and through adoption of clean power, heat and transport technologies. The power sector around the world would need to be at least 60% decarbonised by 2050 for atmospheric concentrations to stabilise at or below 550 ppm CO_2e, and deep emissions cuts will also be required in the transport sector.

Even with very strong expansion of the use of renewable energy and other low-carbon energy sources, fossil fuels could still make up over half of global energy supply in 2050. Coal will continue to be important in the energy mix around the world, including in fast-growing economies. Extensive carbon capture and storage will be necessary to allow the continued use of fossil fuels without damage to the atmosphere.

Cuts in non-energy emissions, such as those resulting from deforestation and from agricultural and industrial processes, are also essential.

With strong, deliberate policy choices, it is possible to reduce emissions in both developed and developing economies on the scale necessary for stabilisation in the required range while continuing to grow.

Climate change is the greatest market failure the world has ever seen, and it interacts with other market imperfections. Three elements of policy are required for an effective global response. The first is the pricing of carbon, implemented through tax, trading, or regulation. The second is policy to support innovation and the deployment of low-carbon technologies. And the third is action to remove barriers to energy efficiency, and to inform, educate, and persuade individuals about what they can do to respond to climate change.

Climate Change Demands an International Response

Many countries and regions are taking action already: the EU [European Union], California and China are among those with the most ambitious policies that will reduce greenhouse gas emissions. The UN [United Nations] Framework Convention on Climate Change and the Kyoto Protocol provide a basis for international co-operation, along with a range of partnerships and other approaches. But more ambitious action is now required around the world.

Countries facing diverse circumstances will use different approaches to make their contribution to tackling climate change. But action by individual countries is not enough. Each country, however large, is just a part of the problem. It is essential to create a shared international vision of long-term goals, and to build the international frameworks that will help each country to play its part in meeting these common goals.

Malawi's Food Security Is Threatened by Climate Change

Singy Hanyona

Singy Hanyona states that the rise of global temperatures directly correlates to the rise of human beings facing hunger and starvation. In Malawi alone, nearly half the population requires food aid due to climate change. Several southern African countries have had to adapt their agricultural processes to deal with drought and rising temperatures. Hanyona reports that rising temperatures and prolonged drought have left farmers in southern Africa to change their traditional farming systems as more of the population faces food shortages.

Singy Hanyona was a member of the African Network of Environmental Journalists until his death in April 2006. Hanyona's self-stated mission was to promote public understanding of environmental issues in Africa by improving the quality, accuracy, and intensity of environmental journalism.

As you read, consider the following questions:

1. Roughly how many Malawians face starvation and require food aid?
2. Name two southern African countries where the farming industry has been affected by global warming.

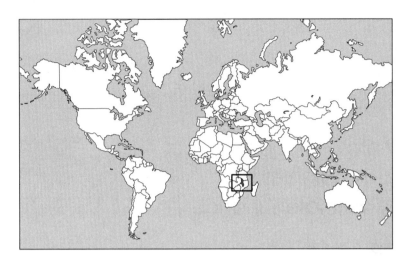

3. Established in 1991, the Global Environment Facility (GEF) does what for developing countries?

Climate changes have led to a drastic fall in agricultural production in Malawi and other southern African countries delegates to the ongoing UN [United Nations] climate change conference are learning. Already overburdened with HIV/AIDS, malaria and tuberculosis, unprecedented drought has hit these countries, pressuring them to import huge amounts of food.

Due to climate change, farmers in Sub-Saharan Africa are no longer certain when the rains will begin and when to plant.

In a moving statement to the Adaptation and Development Seminar at the conference, Lands Secretary George Mkondiwa of Malawi, said the time when Malawians were able to feed themselves, after independence in 1964, is long gone.

"As I speak, some five million Malawians; nearly half of the entire population, face starvation and require food aid," said Mkondiwa. "The more vulnerable sections of the population are subsisting on unpalatable wild foods."

The Development and Adaptation Days event took place Saturday and Sunday [December 2005]. Hosted by the International Institute for Environment and Development, the International Institute for Sustainable Development, and the RING Alliance of Policy Research Organizations, this event was held alongside the 11th Conference of the parties to the UN Framework Convention on Climate Change (UNFCCC) and the first meeting of the parties to its Kyoto Protocol.

Zambian scientist Dr. George Kasali told seminar participants that due to climate change, farmers in Sub-Saharan Africa are no longer certain when the rains will begin and when to plant. He admits that Zambia is among the countries that have been affected by food insecurity as a result of the warming climate.

He said that countries in Sub-Saharan Africa, including Zambia, are in the process of developing a National Adaptation Programme of Action on Climate Change (NAPA); there is a need to engage all stakeholders in the consultative process.

The Food Crisis in Zambia

"We need to organize more activities around the issue of climate change. The role of the media becomes critical in this," said Dr. Kasali, an independent consultant who works with a local environmental group, the Energy and Environmental Concerns of Zambia.

Already, in the southern part of Zambia, food crisis has hit villagers, and an estimated 400,000 people are starving.

Evans Mwengwe, Care International Zambia project manager for food security and agriculture, says agricultural production has declined as a result of many factors, including climate change, that are taking their toll on most Zambian farming communities.

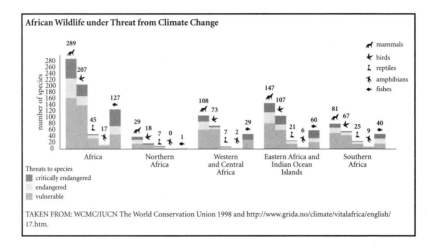

African Wildlife under Threat from Climate Change

TAKEN FROM: WCMC/IUCN The World Conservation Union 1998 and http://www.grida.no/climate/vitalafrica/english/17.htm.

Aaneas Chuma, the UN resident representative for Zambia, confirmed that as a result of the food crisis, Care International has targeted 8,000 households for food aid and also has initiated a K40,000 (US$10), cash transfer program in which villagers are given cash to buy certain commodities. Zambia is currently importing maize [corn], the country's staple food, from the neighboring South Africa.

The Food Crisis in Malawi

In Malawi, Mkondiwa told delegates, last year farmers who planted during the first rains as recommended by agricultural extension scientists, had to helplessly watch their crops scorch and die as rains stopped for long spells. He says the pattern has been the same over several years.

"Everyone is asking such questions as, 'Is this due to climate change or not . . . and what proof do you have?' I can assure you that everyone that is experiencing these adverse effects firsthand, that indeed the patterns and trends in climate have changed in the last decades," Mkondiwa said.

While local scientists have not yet published their findings in the journal *Science*, Mkondiwa told delegates at the Adaptation and Development Seminar, "We don't think there is any doubt that this is due to climate change."

"Malawi does not have the luxury to wait, for instance, for scientific research to prove some indelible link between climate change and recent droughts, because people are dying now," he said.

Most small-scale farmers in southern African countries like Mozambique, Zambia, Malawi and Zimbabwe, have historically been able to adapt to normal climatic variability with creative and indigenous practices. However, the recent droughts have affected these traditional systems and thrown farmers into a state of confusion.

Global Warming Is Affecting Developing Countries in Africa

Most small-scale farmers in southern African countries like Mozambique, Zambia, Malawi and Zimbabwe, have historically been able to adapt to normal climatic variability with creative and indigenous practices. However, the recent droughts have affected these traditional systems and thrown farmers into a state of confusion.

While farmers in the developed world can often make up for short rainy seasons by using man-made water sources, farmers in southern Africa often labor without the most basic of irrigation systems. Burdened by decades of underdevelopment and impoverishment, the agricultural industry so crucial to African economies is now increasingly crippled by periodic droughts.

In addition to its high environmental impact, climate change in Sub-Saharan Africa is made even more dire by the region's limited resources.

The capacity of most developing countries to respond to rapid environmental changes is diminished by infrastructures and budgets already strained by a multitude of competing challenges.

"Climate change does not act in isolation in Africa but, instead, is just one additional stressor, because we are already contending with a lot of problems, including poverty, food insecurity, civil wars and conflicts," said Dr. Anthony Nyong, professor of environmental science at the University of Jos in Nigeria.

Global warming is caused by increased atmospheric levels of greenhouse gases, such as carbon dioxide, methane and nitrous oxide. Industrialization and human activities that burn oil, gasoline and coal push the concentration of these gases in the atmosphere to artificially high levels.

As a result, the average temperature of the earth's surface has risen by 0.6 degrees Celsius over the past 100 years, and will climb by another 1.4 to 5.8 degrees Celsius in the next century, according to the Secretariat of the UN Framework Convention on Climate Change.

The world's most developed countries are the leading producers of greenhouse gases. The United States pumps out about 25 percent of all greenhouse emissions, while the G8 [Group of Eight, an international forum of developed countries] nations together are responsible for about half the world's total output.

By comparison, the entire African continent produces only about 5 percent of all greenhouse gas emissions. . . .

Climate Change Could Be Factored into Development in Africa

The United States Agency for International Development (USAID) is examining how adaptation could be incorporated into specific development projects that are likely to be sensitive to climate change.

In the South African city of Polokwane, formerly Pietersburg, for instance, infrastructure is being built to supply water to the municipality for urban, agricultural, mining and other uses in this semi-arid area, which is already prone to drought.

Much of Mozambique experienced a good cereal and cassava [a starchy root, like potatoes] crop in 2005 compared with other countries in the region. However, the country is suffering from its fourth consecutive year of drought and many thousands are in need of food aid.

Mozambican farmers tend to explain the floods of 2000 and the recent sequence of droughts as the results of supernatural intervention. "They say it is punishment from God, an expression of ancestors' anger or bad luck," says Pablo Suarez, of Boston University, telling the seminar participants about community disaster management.

Suarez said, "As a consequence, they think that these events are unlikely to happen again, therefore, reducing their willingness to set up early warning systems or to replace maize by drought-resistant crops such as cassava."

Suarez sums it up by saying that bringing climate change awareness to rural areas can help Mozambican farmers see that those extreme events may be related to a different, global process.

The Global Environment Facility (GEF) Capacity Development and Adaptation Cluster puts development planning at the apex of preparing for climate change, saying there is need for communities to be better prepared to face the expected challenges of climate change.

Established in 1991, the GEF helps developing countries fund projects and programs that protect the global environment, including projects related to climate change.

The Middle East Faces Water Shortages and Food Scarcity Due to Climate Change

United Nations Office for the Coordination of Humanitarian Affairs

The United Nations (UN) Office for the Coordination of Humanitarian Affairs claims that rising global temperatures will significantly affect food and water security in the Middle East. They predict that shifts in rainfall may directly affect crops, which in turn could raise food prices. Increased food prices or water shortages could economically and politically destabilize the region.

The UN Office for the Coordination of Humanitarian Affairs was formed in 1991 to strengthen the UN's response to natural disasters and emergency situations.

As you read, consider the following questions:

1. What are the four dimensions of food security affected by climate change?
2. What country is the world's second largest importer of wheat and wheat-related products?
3. How many people die from hunger or related illnesses every day across the world?

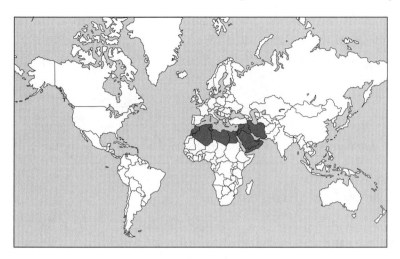

A report by UN [United Nations] Food and Agriculture Organization (FAO), entitled "Climate Change: Implications for Agriculture in the Near East," has said the food security of those who are poor, malnourished or dependent on local food production could be adversely affected by climate change.

"Climate change will affect food security in all its four dimensions—food availability, food accessibility, food stability and food utilisation," Will Killmann, chairman of FAO's working group on climate change, told IRIN on 10 March [2008].

"Food security is particularly threatened in the already vulnerable regions—Sub-Saharan Africa, South Asia and parts of the Middle East," he said.

Shifts in rainfall patterns could affect crops, particularly rice, in many countries in the region, said the FAO report, which has singled out Yemen as being particularly at risk because of its endemic poverty, rapidly growing population and acute water shortages.

High food prices are on everyone's lips across the Middle East. On 3 March [2008] Prime Minister of Bahrain Shaikh Khalifa Bin Salman al-Khalifa used his weekly meeting with officials and ordinary people to address the issue of food security in the region: "We need to draw lessons from the current spiralling inflation hitting the world and start seriously to think about ensuring food security in the Arab world," he said.

Food security experts in the region warn that if regional food prices are not contained social unrest could occur.

Risk of Social Unrest

Food security experts in the region warn that if regional food prices are not contained social unrest could occur. "In principle, increasing food insecurity can trigger resource-based conflict—be it agricultural or be it food," Kilmann said.

Recent incidents in Egypt highlight the vulnerability of the Middle East region to the vagaries of reduced agricultural production and the rise in food prices: Two people were killed as they fought over a place in a queue for cheap, subsidised bread in Helwan, southern Cairo; Egypt's semi-official newspaper *Al Ahram* reported that a man doused a bakery with petrol before setting it alight after its owner refused to sell him bread; and a few days later, on 11 March [2008], *Al Ahram* reported that the number of people who had died in bread queues (so-called "bread martyrs") had reached 10.

Egypt, the world's second largest importer of wheat, subsidises wheat, flour and bread at an annual cost of US$2.74bn to the state. Economists have said the subsidies distort the economy and some within the government have reportedly been talking of a reduction in basic food subsidies. The last time the Egyptian government attempted to do that—in 1977—there were street riots in which the police killed over 70 protesters. Bread prices in Egypt increased by 36.5 percent from February 2007 to February 2008.

In the past few weeks, there have been food riots or demonstrations—albeit on a smaller scale—against rising food prices in a number of countries in the region, including Bahrain, Jordan, Lebanon, Morocco, Saudi Arabia and Yemen. A number of people have died in clashes with security forces. A clash in Beirut on 27 January [2008] between the Lebanese Army and a group of Shia protesters in which seven people were killed started with demonstrations over rising bread prices and power cuts.

On 6 March [2008], while visiting the European Union in Brussels, the executive director of the UN World Food Programme [WFP], Josette Sheeran, warned that high food prices and resulting inflation would continue at least for the next two years, fuelling discontent on the streets of poorer nations.

"Our assessment is that the current level will continue for the next few years . . . in fact rise in 2008 and 2009 and probably [go on] at least until 2010," she said.

"Newly Hungry"

Sheeran mentioned the effects of climate change as being one of the factors that have led to high food prices and what she called the "newly hungry".

"This is leading to a new face of hunger in the world, what we call the newly hungry. These are people who have money, but have been priced out of being able to buy food," she said. "Higher food prices will increase social unrest in a number of countries which are sensitive to inflationary pressures and are import-dependent. We will see a repeat of the riots we have already seen on the streets of Burkina Faso, Cameron and Senegal."

Over 25,000 people die from hunger or related illnesses every day across the world, with one child dying every five seconds, according to WFP.

The situation could, in fact, worsen as FAO has warned that crop growing may become unsustainable in some areas as a result of the complex interactions of myriad factors. It said

Estimated Deaths Attributed to Climate Change in the Year 2000, by Subregion

Change in climate compared to baseline 1961–1990 climate

Mortality per million population

- 0–2
- 2–4
- 4–70
- 70–120
- no data

Maps produced by the Center for Sustainability and the Global Environment (SAGE)

TAKEN FROM: McMichael JJ, Campbell-Lendrum D, Kovats RS, et al. Global Climate Change. In *Comparative Quantification of Health Risks: Global and Regional Burden of Disease due to Selected Major Risk Factors.* M. Ezzati, Lopez AD, Rodgers A, Murray CJL, Geneva World Health Organization, 2004.

maize yields in north Africa, for example, could fall by 15–25 percent with a three degree centigrade rise in temperature.

A number of Gulf states have introduced price controls, including food subsidies and caps on rent increases, to offset the impact of price rises on their populations. The Omani Chamber of Commerce and Industry, for example, proposed on 9 March [2008] that food suppliers should control price rises by introducing ceilings on nine basic food items, including rice, wheat flour, sugar, lentils, cooking oil, tea, milk powder, evaporated milk and ghee [a clarified butter].

Bangladeshis Fear Climate Change Will Bring Stronger Storms, Flooding, and Famine

Fred de Sam Lazaro

In the following transcript, Fred de Sam Lazaro discusses Cyclone Sidr, a severe storm that wrecked havoc along the Bangladesh coast. Water issues are one of the biggest long-term problems facing Bangladesh. Scientists predict rising global temperatures will cause more intense cyclones and as the sea rises, salt water will continue to contaminate the rice fields, creating major food shortages. Bangladesh is currently attempting to find creative solutions to deal with the flooding. Fred de Sam Lazaro is a medical correspondent for PBS's NewsHour *and has won numerous awards for his reporting.*

As you read, consider the following questions:

1. How many people did Cyclone Sidr kill along the Bangladesh coast?
2. What is the biggest problem Bangladeshi farmers face due to climate change?
3. Bangladesh has a landmass the size of Wisconsin (population 5 million). What is the population of Bangladesh?

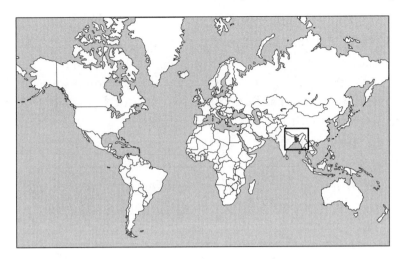

Months after Cyclone Sidr killed 3,200 people along the Bangladesh coast, many of the modest homes still lie in hopeless disrepair.

The human suffering is on fullest display at distribution centers, like this one run by the charity Islamic Relief.

On this day [March 2008], 700 families were given care packages: cooking utensils, toiletries and some basic clothing. Many more went home empty handed.

Sixty-two-year-old Saidur Rahman was among those who took home a bag. His family has gotten some emergency food supplies, scarcely enough to get by. The Rahmans had moved back into their badly damaged house after patching it up. But they say their life is still in tatters because of the death of their 27-year-old son.

SAIDUR RAHMAN: He went out to fish, when the cyclone came he was trying to park his boat but another boat collided with him, he fell in his boat, he was injured and he died.

FRED DE SAM LAZARO: *November's cyclone was the strongest ever recorded in a land that's seen many. Yet the death toll was among the smallest. The previous storm, in 1991, killed 140,000. This time there were early warnings and schools were used as shelters.*

The relief effort, led mostly by international and non-government groups, is helping people put homes together temporarily with corrugated iron sheets. It will take years to build sturdier homes.

With tens of millions of people living no more than 30 feet above sea level, Bangladesh is at ground zero for global warming.

Future of Bangladesh

But the long-term future for the country is a real challenge. Many scientists have said climate change would cause more and more intense cyclones. These farmers have no doubt.

FARMER: It's not just Cyclone. We are facing a disaster every day with water problems.

FRED DE SAM LAZARO: They say salt water from the encroaching sea is contaminating the rice fields in this low lying delta.

FARMER: The crops have reduced productivity and you can see fewer trees grow here. From past years to now, gradually the land is decreasing, going further and further down. We don't really know but it is our guess that the developed countries that have big factories and machinery, they're producing some gases. Those gas mix with the air and that is making the environment polluted.

FRED DE SAM LAZARO: The country's leading climatologist says with tens of millions of people living no more than 30 feet above sea level, Bangladesh is at ground zero for global warming.

ATIQ RAHMAN, Bangladesh Center for Advanced Studies: So, the ocean will rise this way and the central flood plain, which will be inundated more.

Dr. Atiq Rahman says Bangladesh is pummeled from all sides, from the south by cyclones; from the north flow rivers increasingly swollen by melting glaciers in the Himalayas.

FRED DE SAM LAZARO: *So it's making almost like a lake in the middle of the country?*

ATIQ RAHMAN: It already does that every year, certain amount of flooding takes place every year.

FRED DE SAM LAZARO: *In this, the dry season, it's easy to measure the impact of erosion. Like people, the trees struggle to stay rooted. If, as some scientists predict, sea levels rise about three feet by the end of this century, a lot of Bangladesh will, simply, disappear.*

ATIQ RAHMAN: If the sea level rises by a meter, this is the amount the land, below that line south of that line that will disappear, that will go under water.

FRED DE SAM LAZARO: *About a quarter of the landmass.*

ATIQ RAHMAN: About a quarter of the landmass.

FRED DE SAM LAZARO: *It's already happening. In the capital's burgeoning slums, precarious stilts a water mark of the wet season.*

Joynal Mollah moved into this small room four years ago with his wife and four young children, scraping by as laborers on less than two dollars a day. The land his family had farmed for 200 years and the home on it fell into the river.

JOYNAL MOLLAH, laborer: I used to have a piece of land, a third of an acre. We used to have a home, it had a big kitchen. As I lost my land and house in the village, the situation compelled me to come here, otherwise no one would live in a place like this.

FRED DE SAM LAZARO: *The question is, where will all the people driven from their land go?*

Bangladesh Is Running Out of Land

Bangladesh has a landmass approximately the size of Wisconsin, which has a population of about 5 million. Bangladesh's population is 146 million.

Projected Regional Impacts of Climate Change in Asia

- By the 2050s, freshwater availability in Central, South, East and South-East Asia, particularly in large river basins, is projected to decrease.

- Coastal areas, especially heavily populated megadelta regions in South, East and South-East Asia, will be at greatest risk due to increased flooding from the sea and, in some megadeltas, flooding from the rivers.

- Climate change is projected to compound the pressures on natural resources and the environment associated with rapid urbanisation, industrialization, and economic development.

- Endemic morbidity and mortality due to diarrhoeal disease primarily associated with floods and droughts are expected to rise in East, South and South-East Asia due to projected changes in the hydrological cycle.

"Summary for Policy Makers," 2007. www.ipcc.ch.

If the country is running out of land, Mohammad Rezwan says it will have to look to the water.

MOHAMMAD REZWAN, teacher: People have to live on water in some way at the time. And it is the most densely populated country in the world, people they will not have any place to live. It is because of climate change.

FRED DE SAM LAZARO: When Rezwan graduated from architecture school eight years ago, he began to use his skills to design a floating community.

Its first building block was a boat to serve both as school bus—and school.

MOHAMMAD REZWAN: We designed in a way that it has more space and a multi-layered waterproof roof on it so that when it rains you still can continue working on it. And there are side windows and the bottom is flat so it can move through the flooded lands.

FRED DE SAM LAZARO: His fledgling nonprofit caught the attention of donors including the [Bill and Melinda] Gates and Levi Strauss foundations. Today, there are 41 floating, solar-powered classrooms plying the Natore region in northwestern Bangladesh. For 1,200 students, school is no longer interrupted by flooding.

One boat serves as a library. It makes three-hour stops along the river. Its young patrons can study, check out a book, or learn to use the Internet.

There's also a floating power station. Eighty percent of Bangladesh's villages lack electricity. Rezwan provides families solar lamps, powered by small batteries that people bring in about once a month to be recharged.

MOHAMMAD REZWAN: We always had surplus energy on the boat and at the same time the children in the rural houses, they couldn't study during the night. We decided why don't we share our surplus energy with these children? In this way we developed the solar lamp.

FRED DE SAM LAZARO: Rezwan is also trying to help struggling farmers survive on the land they have left.

In a simple assembly line outside his headquarters, used bicycles are, well, recycled into irrigation pumps. They are sold at a 50 percent subsidy to farmers for about twenty-seven U.S. dollars.

MOHAMMAD REZWAN: It is difficult for the landless or marginal farmers to cultivate. Earlier they could get only one crop a year because it is very difficult for them to get the diesel pump. Diesel pump is expensive.

FRED DE SAM LAZARO: The workers he's hired to make the pumps and farmers like Jalal Ahmed have benefited.

JALAL AHMED: Until two years ago, it was very difficult to bring water to the field so we used to bring it up in bowls that we carried. Before using this pump, we used to get only one crop a year. Now I get up to five crops a year because we can irrigate the land.

FRED DE SAM LAZARO: Experts say it will take affordable, so called green technology—bicycle pumps, floating schools and homes—to quite literally keep communities above water, to produce enough food.

The challenge, Dr. Rahman says, is the sheer scale of the problem and population. He says people will be forced to move and he suggests in future treaties that these so called carbon credits should be traded for climate refugees.

ATIQ RAHMAN: So if U.S.A. is producing—a city or enterprise, it's producing so many million tons of carbon, you have to take two villages—villages from Bangladesh. If Switzerland is doing that, take another three villages. You know, that's probably a fair swap, which will not please a lot of people.

FRED DE SAM LAZARO: You're tongue in cheek.

ATIQ RAHMAN: Well, it's a global market and climate change is a global phenomenon, so if humans have to move, they shall find places to move. That's how the Irish moved. That's how the Italians moved. Why not Bangladeshis?

FRED DE SAM LAZARO: Meanwhile, as scientists and relief agencies discuss the long-term effects of climate change, their efforts to deal with them are likely to be hindered by the desperate, immediate needs of victims of this country's increasingly frequent natural disasters.

Small Island States Face Substantial Challenges from Rising Sea Levels

Intergovernmental Panel on Climate Change: Working Group II

The Intergovernmental Panel on Climate Change (IPCC) asserts that small island states located within the tropics are especially vulnerable to climate change due to rising sea levels. The IPCC reports predict that ecosystems such as coral reefs will be affected by rising sea levels and several small island states will face serious freshwater shortages as global temperatures rise. In the Caribbean, where tourism is a major industry, loss of beaches and an increase in tropical storms could severely affect the long-term sustainability of the tourism industry in this and other small island states. The IPCC is the United Nations organization dedicated to bringing together the foremost climactic scientists in order to assess the earth's climate change.

As you read, consider the following questions:

1. Why are low-lying island states considered especially vulnerable to climate change?
2. What are some of the health problems that would be exacerbated by climate change on small island states?
3. What percentage of the Bahamas's gross national product (GNP) is attributed to tourism?

Intergovernmental Panel on Climate Change: Working Group II, "Small Island States," *Climate Change 2007: Impacts, Adaptation and Vulnerability*, pp. 687–90, 2007.

With the exception of Malta and Cyprus in the Mediterranean, all of the small island states considered here are located within the tropics. About one-third of the states comprise a single main island; the others are made up of several or many islands. Low-lying island states and atolls are especially vulnerable to climate change and associated sea-level rise because in many cases (e.g., the Bahamas, Kiribati, the Maldives, the Marshall Islands), much of the land area rarely exceeds 3–4 m [meters] above present mean sea level. Many islands at higher elevation also are vulnerable to climate change effects, particularly in their coastal zones, where the main settlements and vital economic infrastructure almost invariably are concentrated.

Vulnerabilities

Ecosystems: Although projected temperature rise is not anticipated to have widespread adverse consequences, some critical ecosystems, such as coral reefs, are very sensitive to temperature changes. Although some reefs have the ability to keep pace with the projected rate of sea-level rise, in many parts of the tropics (e.g., the Caribbean Sea, the Pacific Ocean) some species of corals live near their limits of temperature tolerance. Elevated seawater temperatures (above seasonal maxima) can seriously damage corals by bleaching and also impair their reproductive functions, and lead to increased mortality. The adaptive capacity of mangroves to climate change is expected to vary by species, as well as according to local conditions (e.g., the presence or absence of sediment-rich, macrotidal environments, the availability of adequate fresh water to maintain the salinity balance). The natural capacity of mangroves to adapt and migrate landward also is expected to be reduced by coastal land loss and the presence of infrastructure in the coastal zone. On some islands, ecosystems already are being harmed by other anthropogenic [caused by humans] stresses (e.g., pollution), which may pose as great a threat as climate change itself. Climate change would add to these stresses and further compromise the long-term viability of these tropical ecosystems.

Hydrology and Water Resources: Freshwater shortage is a serious problem in many small island states, and many such states depend heavily on rainwater as the source of water. Changes in the patterns of rainfall may cause serious problems to such nations.

Coastal Systems: Higher rates of erosion and coastal land loss are expected in many small islands as a consequence of the projected rise in sea level. In the case of Majuro atoll in the Marshall Islands and Kiribati, it is estimated that for a 1-m [meter] rise in sea level as much as 80% and 12.5% (respectively) of total land would be vulnerable. Generally, beach sediment budgets are expected to be adversely affected by reductions in sediment deposition. On high islands, however, increased sediment yield from streams will help to compensate for sand loss from reefs. Low-lying island states and atolls also are expected to experience increased sea flooding, inundation, and salinization (of soils and freshwater lenses) as a direct consequence of sea-level rise.

Human Settlements and Infrastructure: In a number of islands, vital infrastructure and major concentrations of settlements are likely to be at risk, given their location at or near present sea level and their proximity to the coast (often within 1–2 km [kilometers]; e.g., Kiribati, Tuvalu, the Maldives, the Bahamas). Moreover, vulnerability assessments also suggest that shore and infrastructure protection costs could be financially burdensome for some small island states.

Human Health: Climate change is projected to exacerbate health problems such as heat-related illness, cholera, dengue fever, and biotoxin poisoning, and would place additional stress on the already over-extended health systems of most small islands.

Climate Change Emigrants Leave Tuvalu

Regions likely to bear the brunt of climate impacts are already beginning to look to neighbouring states for potential resettlement. According to IPCC [Intergovernmental Panel on Climate Change] projections, global average sea level will rise between 18–59 centimetres by 2100, but some estimates say that could be as much as 1.4 metres. Future evacuation is probable for some low-lying Pacific islands vulnerable to sea-level rise and extreme-weather intensity. In recent years, they have initiated discussions with their neighbours Australia and New Zealand about possible safe migration routes to nearby countries on higher ground. The government of Tuvalu, a Polynesian island nation with a population of some 12,000, negotiated an agreement with New Zealand to accept 75 Tuvaluan immigrants annually, a program that began in 2002. So far, Australia has not agreed to a similar resettlement deal. Yet despite the potential exit strategies, some believe that the focus should be on securing the sovereignty and the rights of societies that will be impacted by climate change. "Migration from the Pacific and from small-island states as an adaptation option is missing the point," says Jon Barnett, a political geographer at the University of Melbourne, Australia. "Adaptation should aim to protect the rights of people to live in their home."

Amanda Leigh Haag,
"Is This What the World's Coming To?"
Nature, *2007. www.nature.com.*

Tourism: Tourism is the dominant economic sector in a number of small island states in the Caribbean Sea and the Pacific and Indian Oceans. In 1995, tourism accounted for 69%, 53%, and 50% of gross national product (GNP) in Antigua, the Bahamas, and the Maldives, respectively. This sector also earns considerable foreign exchange for a number of small island states, many of which are heavily dependent on imported food, fuel, and a range of other vital goods and services. Foreign exchange earnings from tourism also provided more than 50% of total revenues for some countries in 1995. Climate change and sea-level rise would affect tourism directly and indirectly: Loss of beaches to erosion and inundation, salinization of freshwater aquifers, increasing stress on coastal ecosystems, damage to infrastructure from tropical and extra-tropical storms, and an overall loss of amenities would jeopardize the viability and threaten the long-term sustainability of this important industry in many small islands.

On some small low-lying island states and atolls . . . retreat away from the coasts is not an option . . . migration and resettlement outside of national boundaries might have to be considered.

Conclusions: To evaluate the vulnerability of these island states to projected climate change, a fully integrated approach to vulnerability assessments is needed. The interaction of various biophysical attributes (e.g., size, elevation, relative isolation) with the islands' economic and sociocultural character ultimately determines the vulnerability of these islands. Moreover, some islands are prone to periodic non-climate related hazards (e.g., earthquakes, volcanic eruptions, tsunamis); the overall vulnerability of these islands cannot be accurately evaluated in isolation from such threats. Similarly, vulnerability assessments for these small island states should take into consideration the value of non-marketed goods and services (e.g., subsistence assets, community structure, traditional skills and knowledge), which also may be at risk from climate change. In some island societies, these assets are just as important as marketed goods and services.

Uncertainties in climate change projections may discourage adaptation, especially because some options may be costly or require changes in societal norms and behavior. As a guiding principle, policies and development programs which seek to use resources in a sustainable manner, and which can respond effectively to changing conditions such as climate change, would be beneficial to the small island states, even if climate change did not occur.

The small island states are extremely vulnerable to global climate change and global sea-level rise. A range of adaptation strategies is theoretically possible. On some small low-lying island states and atolls, however, retreat away from the coasts is not an option. In some extreme cases, migration and resettlement outside of national boundaries might have to be considered.

South America's Amazon Basin Faces Loss of Animal Species and Habitats

Michael Case

In the following article, Michael Case evaluates scientific reports on the effects of climate change on the Amazon River basin, which contains a huge portion of the world's biodiversity. The research consolidated here discusses climate change's likely effects on the thousands of species of plants, animals, and insects that make their homes in the Amazon region.

Michael Case is a research scientist for the World Wildlife Fund (WWF) Climate Change Programme. The WWF is the largest multinational conservation organization in the world; WWF works in 100 countries and is supported worldwide by 5 million members.

As you read, consider the following questions:

1. Roughly how many different types of amphibians live in the Amazon basin?

2. How many tributaries does the Amazon River support?

3. What native Amazon plant is particularly fire-prone due to the high content of volatile oils in the leaves and bark?

Michael Case, "Climate Change Impacts in the Amazon: Review of Scientific Literature," 2006. http://assets.panda.org. Reproduced by permission.

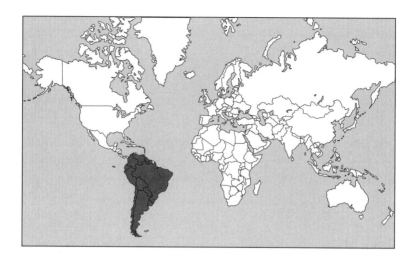

The Amazon

The Amazon basin contains a staggering portion of the world's biodiversity, supports thousands of people through agriculture and silviculture, and provides the world with commodity and non-commodity products such as building supplies and medicine. The Amazon contains one of Earth's richest assortments of biodiversity with recent compilations indicating at least 40,000 plant species, 427 mammals, 1294 birds, 378 reptiles, 427 amphibians, 3,000 fishes, and likely over a million insect species. The Amazon River is the largest single source of freshwater runoff on Earth, representing some 15 to 20% of global river flow (Salati and Vose, 1984). Subsequently, the Amazon's hydrological cycle is a key driver of global climate, and global climate is therefore sensitive to changes in the Amazon. Climate change threatens to substantially affect the Amazon region, which in turn is expected to alter global climate and increase the risk of biodiversity loss.

Observed Climatic Change and Variability

The climate in northwestern South America, including the Amazon region, has already changed over the last century. The monthly mean air temperature records show a warming of

0.5–0.8°C for the last decade of the 20th century (Pabón, 1995a; Pabón et al., 1999; Quintana-Gomez, 1999). In the Amazon region specifically, a warming trend of +0.63°C per 100 years was detected by Victoria et al. (1998). Precipitation trends in the Amazon are not as clear, and multidecadal rainfall variations have shown opposite tendencies in the northern and southern portions of the basin (Marengo et al., 2000). The period 1950–1976 was regionally wet in northern Amazonia, and since 1977 the region has been drier (IPCC, 2001), suggesting the affect of long-term climatic variability.

Recent studies have clarified the link between deforestation and precipitation in the Amazon. Chagnon and Bras (2005) found that current deforestation causes a dramatic change in climatological rainfall occurrence patterns; high-resolution satellite precipitation measurements show significantly more rainfall occurrence over deforested areas. They also found a long-term shift in the seasonality of precipitation that correlates with deforestation, suggesting the two are closely associated. Rainfall accumulations have decreased significantly at the end of the wet season, and have increased at the end of the dry season (Chagnon and Bras, 2005). These findings imply that current deforestation in the Amazon has already altered the regional climate and support previous findings of enhanced shallow cloudiness over deforested areas (Chagnon et al., 2004). However, earlier findings suggest more widespread changes; studies have shown a decadal intensification of precipitation over the entire Amazon (Chu et al., 1994; DeLiberty, 2000; Chen et al., 2002).

El Niño/Southern Oscillation (ENSO) seems to be a driver of much of the climatic variability in Latin America (IPCC, 2001). For example, El Niño is associated with dry conditions in northeast Brazil, northern Amazonia, the Peruvian-Bolivian Altiplano, and Pacific coast of Central America. The most severe droughts in Mexico in recent decades have occurred during El Niño years, whereas southern Brazil and northwestern

Peru have exhibited anomalously wet conditions at these times (Horel and Cornejo Garrido, 1986). La Niña is associated with heavy precipitation and flooding in Colombia and drought in southern Brazil (Rao et al., 1986).

Climate change effects pose a substantial threat to Amazonian forests and the biodiversity within them. Amazonian forests contain a large portion of the world's biodiversity; at least 12% of all flowering plants are found within the Amazon therefore threats to Amazon forests translate into threats to biodiversity at large.

Predicted Climatic Change

General Circulation Models (GCM's) project a regional increase of 2–3°C by the year 2050 and a decrease in precipitation in the Amazon during dry months, leading to widespread drying (Mitchell et al., 1995; Kattenberg et al., 1996). Ecosystem models that use expected climatic changes show large declines in net primary productivity (NPP) and release of carbon as a result of Amazonian forest dieback (Friend et al., 1997). In fact, climate change effects may change the current status of Amazonian forests from a net sink of atmospheric CO_2 [carbon dioxide] into a source, which will further contribute to dangerous levels of atmospheric CO_2 (IPCC, 2001). GCM's also suggest that a globally warmer world may result in a permanent El Niño-like state (Wara et al., 2005), which if manifested by drought conditions, could have huge impacts on the Amazon.

Impacts

Empirical and modeled data suggest that the Amazon basin is at particular risk to climate change effects. Projected changes of warmer temperatures and decreased precipitation during already dry months could manifest in longer and perhaps, more severe droughts and substantial changes in seasonality. Coupled with land use changes, these changes could lead to devastating impacts, including; increased erosion, degradation of freshwater systems, loss of ecologically and agriculturally valuable soils, loss of biodiversity, decreased agricultural yields, increased insect infestation, and spread of infectious diseases.

Forests

Climate change effects pose a substantial threat to Amazonian forests and the biodiversity within them. Amazonian forests contain a large portion of the world's biodiversity; at least 12% of all flowering plants are found within the Amazon (Gentry, 1982) therefore threats to Amazon forests translate into threats to biodiversity at large. In fact, climate modeling studies have projected a warming and drying effect, which when combined with a decrease in evapotranspiration from plants will likely lead to a substantial decrease in precipitation over much of the Amazon. These changes will likely lead to significant shifts in ecosystem types and loss of species in many parts of the Amazon (Miles et al., 2004; Markham, 1998). Land-use change will also interact with climate through positive feedback processes that will accelerate the loss of Amazon forests (IPCC, 2001).

At the biome level, GCMs of potential future climates project that evergreen forests are succeeded by mixed forest, savanna and grassland in eastern Amazonia and savanna expand into parts of western Amazonia (Cramer et al., 2001; Cramer et al., 2004). Other modeling experiments project an expansion of savanna, grasslands and desert ecosystems into north-eastern Amazonia (White et al., 1999). Large-scale modeling shows widespread forest loss over most of the Amazon, accelerated by positive feedback between warming, forest dieback, and emissions of carbon from soil and vegetation (White et al., 1999; Cox et al., 2000; Jones et al. 2003; Cox et al., 2004). In fact, the Brazilian government has released figures suggesting that deforestation has exceeded 520,000 square km [kilometers] since 1978, with the second worst year of forest loss occurring in 2004 (National Institute for Space Research, 2005). Species specific modeling suggests that 43% sampled Amazon plant species may become non-viable by the year 2095 because their potential distributions will have changed due to climatic shifts (Miles et al., 2004). In order for species affected by these changes to reach appropriate new bioclimatic zones, dispersal or migration would have to occur over hundreds of kilometers (Hare, 2003).

Many of the aforementioned modeling experiments have not considered non-climate influences such as land use, deforestation, water availability, pests and diseases, and fire, all of which may limit the migration and dispersal of tropical forest species. The IPCC suggests that the combination of forces driving deforestation makes it unlikely that tropical forests will be permitted to expand into climatically suitable habitats that are created by climate change.

Amazon forests are also threatened by secondary effects of climate change, such as a potential increase in the frequency and perhaps in intensity of fires. It is suggested that fire poses the greatest threat to Amazon forests and numerous studies have shown a well established link between forest fires, habitat fragmentation, climate change, and extreme El Niño events in the Amazon (Nepstad et al., 2001; Laurance and Williamson, 2001; Laurance et al., 2001; Nepstad et al., 2001; Cochrane and Laurance, 2002).

As mentioned previously climate models predict that a globally warmer world may result in a permanent El Niño-like state (Wara et al., 2005) with dramatic effects such as; droughts, fires, and increased release of carbon to the atmosphere. El Niño events (the positive phase of the El Niño/ Southern Oscillation (ENSO)) tend to dry affected areas and lead to large, intense droughts and fires. Severe droughts can also stress and potentially kill sensitive plant species, resulting in a replacement of tropical moist forests with drought-tolerant plant species (Shukla et al., 1990). It has also been shown that there are substantial releases of carbon from the Amazon during El Niño years (Tian et al., 1998). Strong El Niño years bring hot, dry weather to much of the Amazon region and the ecosystems act as a source of carbon to the atmosphere instead of a sink as during non-El Niño years (Tian et al., 1998).

There are a number of positive feedback loops that drive the expansion of fires in the Amazon: 1) Forest fires release substantial amounts of smoke into the atmosphere which can reduce rainfall and thus promote more drought and more fires (Rosenfeld, 1999); 2) Fire-assisted conversion of forests to agriculture and pastures also promotes drought by decreasing water vapor flux (evapotranspiration) to the atmosphere, further inhibiting rainfall (Nepstad et al., 2001); and 3) Fire increases the susceptibility of forests to recurrent burning by killing trees, thereby allowing sunlight to penetrate and dry the forest interior, and increasing the fuel load on the forest floor (Nepstad et al., 2001).

Human activities such as deforestation, logging, and settlement obviously work in tandem with climate change and increase the drying effect that leads to forest fires. For example, mortality of trees, which increases the fuel load for fire, has been observed to increase under dry conditions that prevail near newly formed edges in Amazonian forests from land clearing and harvesting (IPCC, 2001). Edges, which affect an increasingly large portion of the forest with the advance of deforestation, are especially susceptible to the effects of reduced rainfall and are increasingly susceptible to fire.

Freshwater

The Amazon River, with more than 1000 tributaries, discharges into the Atlantic Ocean some 209,000 cubic meters of water per second (about 60 times the rate of the Nile), which repre-

U.S. Climate Policy Could Help Save Rain Forests

REDD, or Reducing Emissions from Deforestation and Degradation, is a proposed policy mechanism that would compensate tropical countries for safeguarding their forests. Because deforestation accounts for around a fifth of global greenhouse gas emissions, efforts to reduce deforestation can help fight climate change. Forest protection also offers ancillary benefits like the preservation of ecosystem services, biodiversity, and a homeland for indigenous people.

While REDD was excluded from the Kyoto Protocol, policy makers meeting in Bali [Indonesia] last December [2007] signaled that forestry would play a role in future emissions mitigation schemes. The news was welcomed by a coalition of rainforest nations which had been lobbying for the concept and some environmentalists, who see it as a way to make forest conservation pay for itself. Rural populations would also stand to benefit from the initiative.

Rhett Butler,
"U.S. Climate Policy Could Help Save Rainforests,"
May 14, 2008. www.mongabay.com.

sents more than 15% of all the fresh water entering the oceans each day. The average rainfall in the Amazon basin is about 2,300 mm per year and the Amazon River plays an important role in the water cycle and water balance of much of South America. Changes in water regime such as the quantity, quality, and timing can affect the habitats and behavior of many plant and animal species (Hare, 2003), in addition to extremes caused by climatic perturbations in water cycling. Changes in total precipitation, extreme rainfall events, and seasonality will affect the amount, timing, and variability of flow. Changes in total volume or timing of runoff may result in increased or decreased intermittency, while altered volume, variability, and extremes of runoff may affect timing, frequency and severity of flash flooding (Carpenter et al., 1992). Such changes in magnitude and temporal distribution of extreme events may disrupt ecosystems more than changes in mean conditions.

Water and aquatic resources provide many essential services to the people of the Amazon. The region's native fisheries provide a large proportion of animal protein consumed by inhabitants. Fish are also a valuable source of income to fishermen. River and lake water satisfies nearly all of the water supply needs of Amazonian peoples, including drinking, cooking, bathing, and waste removal. While little water is used for irrigation, river channels and lakes are important avenues of transportation and shipping and provide opportunities for recreation (McClain, 2001).

Climate change threatens the Amazon's water regime and freshwater ecosystems because warming temperatures will result in greater evaporation from water surfaces and greater transpiration by plants, which will result in a more vigorous water cycle (Allen et al., 2005). If projected declines in precipitation during dry months occur, climate change impacts to the Amazonian water regime may be exacerbated (Nijssen et al., 2001). Climate change threats to Amazonian freshwater ecosystems are varied, but include:

1) **Warming water temperatures** because of global warming will impact temperature dependent species. Temperature tolerances often govern both the local and biogeographic distribution limits of freshwater fishes (Carpenter et al., 1992). Distributions of aquatic species will likely change as some species invade more high altitude habitats or disappear from the low altitudinal limits of their distribution. Elevated temperatures may also result in reduced water dissolved oxygen concentrations, which may have immediate adverse effects on eggs and larvae, which rely on dissolved oxygen for survival

(Carpenter et al., 1992). Increased water temperatures and reduced precipitation may also reduce suitable habitat during dry, warm summer months and potentially lead to increased exotic species. Exotic fish species often out-compete native species for habitat and food resources and lead to declines in native populations and decreased species diversity (Latini and Petrere Jr, 2004).

2) Decreased precipitation during dry months will affect many Amazonian streams and freshwater systems. Small, shallow habitats (ponds, headwater streams, marshes, and small lakes) will likely experience the first effects of reduced precipitation (Carpenter et al., 1992). While prospects for successful relocation of spawning activities for fishes exist, some may be thwarted by the strong imprinting and homing behavior present in many species.

3) Changes in nutrient input into streams and rivers because of altered forest productivity can greatly affect aquatic organisms. Forested streams are highly dependent upon inputs of terrestrial organic matter, especially leaf fall, because of their nutrient supply. Shifts in terrestrial vegetation and changes in leaf chemistry will impact stream biota and ecosystems. In fact, several climate modeling studies and field experiments show that about 50% of the rainfall in the Amazon region originates as water recycled in the forest.

4) Climate models project a future that has a **more variable climate and more extreme** events (IPCC, 2001), and local fish populations will more often experience extreme events such as those that produce lethal conditions for short periods of time. Such disturbances can deplete stocks of adult fish and other biota, disrupt ecological processes, and redistribute resources (Lake et al., 2000). Even short-lived stresses such as temporary climatic extremes can cascade throughout the trophic network for extended periods. Fish adapted to cooler water temperatures are most vulnerable to climatic extremes such as warm water conditions because they rely on constant temperatures. Relatively modest changes in the weather can dramatically increase variability in recruitment (Cushing, 1982). A cascade of food web effects can follow from the removal or enhancement of fishes whose effects as predators cause variability in the trophic structure, productivity, and water quality of lakes (Carpenter, 1988; Carpenter et al., 1985). Recreational and commercial fisheries are particularly at risk of climate extremes and increased variability because fish populations are notoriously variable, and fisheries yields are often heavily dependent on the occasional strong year class (Pitcher and Hart, 1982). Survival during early life history stages is a key to recruitment success (Wooton, 1990), and the expected increase in climatic variability may lead to variable reproductive success in individual cohorts, which will have immediate social and economic effects (Carpenter et al., 1992). For example, fishermen in the River Tocantins have chosen capture strategies specific to seasonal variations in fish behavior and reproduction (Welcomme, 1985) and changes in climatic spatio-temporal variability could cause these species to decline in numbers or become extinct. Changes in seasonal fluctuations may change the migratory pattern and ecology of fish species and lead to changes in fish catches (Cetra and Petrere Jr, 2001).

Climate change will threaten human health in the Amazon. However, health impacts will vary in magnitude due to the size, density, location, and wealth of the population and are not uniform.

Agriculture

The IPCC (2001) suggests that projected warmer temperatures and changes in precipitation will undoubtedly impact the agricultural sector (including plantation forestry) in the Amazon. Particularly hard hit will be subsidence farming. In fact, agriculture is the basis of subsistence lifestyles and is the largest user of human capital rural communities that are situated within the Amazon. In these areas, agriculture is the main producing sector and it will be severely affected by climatic change and variability (Rosenzweig and Hillel, 1998). A reduction in rainfall during critical dry months may also lead to increased evapotranspiration and pest infestation, which will undoubtedly negatively impact agricultural yields (IPCC, 2001). Climatic change would subsequently require larger areas of land to meet the current levels of demand. In fact, Fearnside (1999) predicts that the total plantation area will have to increase up to 4.5 times the 1991 area by 2050.

Climate change effects on agricultural yields vary by region and by crop. Under certain conditions, the positive physiological effects of CO_2 enrichment could be countered by temperature increases—leading to shortening of the growth season and changes in precipitation, with consequent reductions in crop yields (IPCC 2001). In fact, reduced availability of water and warmer temperatures are expected to have negative effects on wheat, maize, and potentially soybean production in Brazil (de Siqueira et al., 1994). However, it should be noted that there are relatively few agricultural climate change impact studies have been done in South America, especially the Amazon.

Subsistence farming in the Amazon is particularly threatened by potential consequences of climate change. In fact, Rosenzweig et al. (1993) identifies northeastern Brazil as suffering yield impacts that are among the most severe in the world (also see Reilly et al., 1996; Canziani et al., 1998; Rosenzweig and Hillel, 1998). In addition, northeastern Brazil is home to more than 45 million people and is prone to periodic droughts and famines even in the absence of expected climate changes, and any changes in this region would have major consequences for human populations.

Plantation farming, or silviculture, will be greatly impacted by the potential decrease in precipitation caused by climate change in Amazonia. Because water often limits tree growth during the dry season, a decrease in rainfall will have negative impacts on growth and yield. To quantify this effect, Ferraz (1993) has developed a regression equation to approximate the effects of precipitation changes on plantation yields. General circulation climate modeling using the UKMO model (Gates et al., 1992) indicates that annual rainfall changes for regions of Brazil would cause silvicultural yields to decrease by 6% in Amazonia and 8% in southern Brazil. During the June–July–August rainfall period, yields would decrease by 12% in Amazonia, 14% in southern Brazil, and 21% in the northeast (Fearnside, 1999). However, the climate modeling effects on yield are likely to underestimate the true effect of climate change because other secondary climate factors may reduce yield substantially more (i.e., pest and diseases infestation) (Cammell and Knight, 1992). Reduced rainfall may also lead to increased fire risk in plantations, also affecting yield. For example, Eucalyptus is particularly fire-prone because of the high content of volatile oils in the leaves and bark.

CO_2 enrichment may be beneficial for plantations because higher atmospheric concentrations of CO_2 increase the water-use efficiency of some species (i.e., Eucalyptus). While the photosynthetic and nitrogen fixation rates increase (thus lowering the fertilizer demands of plantations) in some Eucalyptus species increased when exposed to high concentrations of CO_2 (Hall et al., 1992), other factors such as reduced water availability, insect, disease, and fire effects are typically not considered and may result in a net negative response to climate change.

Larger areas of plantations (at a higher cost) will likely be needed to meet current levels of demand in a globally warmer world. Fearnside (1999) modeled rainfall reductions of 5, 10, 25, and 50% (all possible climate change scenarios), and calculated the required plantation area would need to increase as much as 38% to meet demands.

Climate models predict that a globally warmer world may result in a permanent El Niño-like state (Wara et al., 2005) and this would have substantial effects on agriculture. Because El Niño events tend to dry impacted areas and lead to large, intense droughts and fires, crops will likely be impacted.

Health

Climate change will threaten human health in the Amazon. However, health impacts will vary in magnitude due to the size, density, location, and wealth of the population and are not uniform (WHO 1998). Human death and mortality rates (injuries, infectious diseases, social problems, and damage to sanitary infrastructure), due to heatwaves, droughts, fires, and floods increased for most of the climate change scenarios that have been modeled from baseline climate conditions in Latin America. However, most modeling has examined urban populations, which because of the poor housing conditions (crowded and poorly ventilated) they are particularly vulnerable to temperature extremes (Kilbourne, 1989; Martens, 1998). Furthermore, the effects of extreme temperature may be significantly different for rural populations (Martens, 1998).

In addition to the already established relationship between extreme temperatures and increased death rates (McMichael et al., 1996), other climate change impacts such as increased occurrence of extreme weather events (e.g., floods, droughts, fire, heatwaves). It has been found that some extreme weather events, such as floods, may be responsible for outbreaks of vector-borne diseases such as malaria and dengue (Moreira, 1986; PAHO, 1998a,b) and for outbreaks of infectious diseases such as cholera and meningitis (Patz, 1998). El Niño and La Niña can also cause changes in disease—vector populations and the incidence of water-borne diseases (Epstein et al., 1998). During droughts, the risk of wildfires increases and the direct effects on human health occur from burns and smoke inhalation (Kovats et al., 1999), in addition to indirect effects from air pollution, primarily from smoke and suspended particles, which can lead to loss of forests, property, livestock, and human life (OPS, 1998). Typically not lethal, increased temperature may lead to an increase in the distribution and growth of allergenic plants. In fact, higher temperatures and lower rainfall at the time of pollen dispersal are likely to result in higher concentrations of airborne pollen during the peak season (Emberlin, 1994; Rosas et al., 1989). Consequently, people who are already sensitive to pollen could be substantially impacted by increased temperature and potential drying of the Amazon and others may develop allergies due to the increased concentrations.

Sea Level Rise

The IPCC suggests that flooding associated with sea-level rise will have substantial impact in lowland areas such as the Amazon River delta. In fact, according to the IPCC (2001), the rate of sea-level rise over the last 100 years in has been 1.0–2.5 mm a year and this rate could now rise to 5 mm per year. Increased temperature, changes in precipitation and runoff, and sea-level rise will have significant impacts on the present habitats of mangroves and create new tidally inundated. Sea-level rise would eliminate mangrove habitat at an approximate rate of 1% yr^{-1}. This effect will cause species composition shifts and will likely affect the region's fisheries that depend on mangrove habitat as nurseries and refuge. For example, commercial shellfish and finfish use mangroves for nurseries and refuge, and a direct relationship of mangrove decline and fisheries decline has been identified in these systems (Martínez et al., 1995; Ewel and Twilley, 1998). The potential disappearance of some mangrove forests could undermine the livelihoods of local fishing communities. Coastal inundation stemming from sea-level rise will also affect water availability (i.e., saltwater intrusion could affect estuaries and freshwater sources) and agricultural land suitability, therefore exacerbating the socio-economic and health problems in sensitive areas (IPCC, 2001).

References:

Allan, J.D., M.A. Palmer and N.L. Poff. 2005. Climate change and freshwater ecosystems. Pp. 272-290. *In* T.E. Lovejoy and L. Hannah (*eds.*), Climate Change and Biodiversity. Yale University Press, New Haven CT., USA.

Cammell, M.E. and J.D. Knight. 1992. Effects of climatic change on the population dynamics of crop pests. Advances in Ecological Research 22: 117-162.

Canziani, O.F., S. Díaz, E. Calvo, M. Campos, R. Carcavallo, C.C. Cerri, C. Gay-García, L.J. Mata, A. Saizar, P. Aceituno, R. Andressen, V. Barros, M. Cabido, H. Fuenzalida-Ponce, G. Funes, C. Galvão, A.R. Moreno, W.M. Vargas, E.F.Viglizao, and M. de Zuviría. 1998. Latin America. *In*: The Regional Impacts of Climate Change: An Assessment of Vulnerability. Special Report of IPCC Working Group II [Watson, R.T., M.C. Zinyowera, and R.H. Moss (*eds.*)]. Intergovernmental Panel on Climate Change, Cambridge University Press, Cambridge, United Kingdom and New York, NY, USA, pp. 187-230.

Carpenter, S. R., (ed.) 1988. Complex Interactions in Lake Communities. New York: Springer-Verlag. 283 pp.

Carpenter, S. R., Kitchell, J. F., Hodgson, J. R. 1985. Cascading trophic interactions and lake productivity. Bio-Science 35:634-39.

Carpenter, S.R. Fisher, S.G., Grimm, N.B., and Kitchell, J.F. 1992. Global change and freshwater ecosystems. Annual Reviews Ecology and Systematics 23: 119-139.

Cetra, M. and Petrere Jr, M. 2001. Small-scale fisheries in the middle River Tocantins, Imperatriz (MA), Brazil Fisheries Management and Ecology 8(2): 153-162.

Chagnon, F. J. F., and R. L. Bras. 2005. Contemporary climate change in the Amazon. Geophysical Research Letters 32: L13703, doi: 10.1029/2005GL022722.

Chagnon, F. J. F., R. L. Bras, and J. Wang. 2004. Climatic shift in patterns of shallow clouds over the Amazon, Geophysical Research Letters 31: L24212, doi: 10.1029/ 2004GL021188.

Chen, J., B. E. Carlson, and A. D. Del Genio. 2002. Evidence for strengthening of the tropical general circulation in the 1990s. Science 295: 838-841.

Chu, P.-S., Z.-P. Yu, and S. Hastenrath. 1994. Detecting climate change concurrent with deforestation in the Amazon basin: Which way has it gone? Bulletin of the American Meteorology Society 75: 579-583.

Cochrane, M. A., and W. F. Laurance. 2002. Fire as a large-scale edge effect in Amazonian forests. Journal of Tropical Ecology 18: 311-325.

Conde, C., D. Liverman, M. Flores, R. Ferrer, R. Araujo, E. Betancourt, G. Villareal, and C. Gay, 1997. Vulnerability of rainfed maize crops in Mexico to climate change. Climate Research 9: 17-23.

Cox, P.M., R.A. Betts. C.D. Jones, S.A. Spall, and I.J. Totterdell. 2000. Acceleration of global warming due to carbon-cycle feedbacks in a coupled climate model. Nature 408: 184-187.

Cox, M.P., R. A. Betts, M. Collins, P.P. Harris, C. Huntingford,and C. D. Jones. 2004. Amazonian forest dieback under climate-carbon cycle projections for the 21st century. Theoretical and Applied Climatology 78: 137-156.

Cramer W., A. Bondeau, S. Schaphoff, W. Lucht, B. Smith, S. Sitch. 2004. Tropical forests and the global carbon cycle:

impacts of atmospheric carbon dioxide, climate change and rate of deforestation. Philosophical Transactions: Biological Sciences 359 (1443): 331-343.

Cramer, W., Bondeau, A., Woodward, F.I., Prentice. I.C., Betts, R.A., Brovkin, V., Cox, J., Fisher, V., Foley, J.A., Friend, A.D., Kucharik, C., Lomas, M.R., Ramankutty, N., Sitch, S., Smith, B., White. A. & Young-Molling, C. 2001. Global response of terrestrial ecosystem structure and function to CO_2 and climate change: results from six dynamic global vegetation models. Global Change Biology 7: 357-373.

Cushing, D.H. 1982. Climate and Fisheries. London: Academic.

Deliberty, T. L. 2000. A regional scale investigation of climatological tropical convection and precipitation in the Amazon basin. Professional geographer 52: 258-271.

deSiqueira, O.J.F., J.R.B. Farías, and L.M.A. Sans, 1994. Potential effects of global climate change for Brazilian agriculture: applied simulation studies for wheat, maize and soybeans. *In*: Implications of Climate Change for International Agriculture: Crop Modeling Study [Rosenzweig, C. and A. Iglesias (*eds.*)]. EPA 230-B-94-003, U.S. Environmental Protection Agency, Washington, DC, USA.

Emberlin, J., 1994. The effects of patterns in climate and pollen abundance on allergy. Allergy 49: 15-20.

Epstein, P.R., H.F. Díaz, S. Elias, O. Grabherr, N.E. Graham, W.J.M. Martens, E. Mosley-Thompson, and J. Susskind. 1998. Biological and physical signs of climate change: focus on mosquito-borne diseases. Bulletin of the American Meteorological Society 79(3): 409-417.

Ewell, K.C. and R.R. Twilley, 1998. Different kinds of mangrove forests provide different goods and services. Global Ecology and Biogeography Letters 7(1): 83-94.

Fearnside, P.M., 1999. Plantation forestry in Brazil: the potential impacts of climatic change. *Biomass and Bioenergy* 16(2): 91-102.

Ferraz, E.S.B. 1993. Influência da precipitação na produção de matería seca de eucalipto. IPEF Piracicaba 46: 32-42 (in Portuguese).

Friend, A.D., AK. Stevens, R.G. Knox, and M.G.R. Cannell, 1997: A process based, terrestrial biosphere model of ecosystem dynamics (hybrid v. 3.0). *Ecological Modelling*, 95, 249-287.

Gates, W.L., J.F.B. Mitchell, G.J. Boer, U. Cubasch, and V.P. Meleshko. 1992. Climate modelling, climate prediction and model validation. *In*: Climate Change 1992: The Supplementary Report to the IPCC Scientific Assessment [Houghton. J.T., B.A. Callander; and S.K. Varney (*eds.*)]. Cambridge University Press. Cambridge, United Kingdom and New York, NY, USA, pp. 97–134.

Gentry, A.H. 1982. Neotropical floristic diversity. Annals of the Missouri Botanical Garden. 69: 557-593.

Hall, D.O., R. Rosillo-Calle, R.H. Williams, and J. Woods, 1992. Biomass for energy: supply prospects. *In*: Renewable Energy: Sources for Fuels and Electricity [Johansson, T.B., H. Kelly, A.K.N. Reddy, and R.H. Williams (*eds.*)]. Island Press, Covelo, CA, USA, pp. 593-651.

Hare, W. 2003. Assessment of Knowledge on Impacts of Climate Change—Contribution to the Specification of Art. 2 of the UNFCCC. WBGU Potsdam, Berlin.

Horel, J. D. and Cornejo-Garrido, A. G. 1986. Convection along the Coast of Northern Peru during 1983: Spatial and temporal variations of clouds and rainfall. Monitor. Weather Rev. 114: 2091–2105.

IPCC, 2001. Climate Change 2001: Impacts, Adaptation, and Vulnerability. Contribution of Working Group II to the Third Assessment Report of the Intergovernmental Panel on Climate Change. Cambridge University Press, Cambridge, UK, 1032p.

IPCC, 2001b.Climate Change 2001: The Scientific Basis. Contribution of Working Group I to the Third Assessment Report of the Intergovernmental Panel on Climate Change. Cambridge University Press, Cambridge, UK, 881p.

Jones, C. D., P. M. Cox, R. L. H. Essery, D. L. Roberts, and M. J. Woodage. 2003. Strong carbon cycle feedbacks in a climate model with interactive CO_2 and sulphate aerosols. Geophysical Research Letters 30(9): 1479.

Kattenberg, A., F. Giorgi, H. Grassl, G.A. Meehl, J.F.B. Mitchell, RJ. Stouffer, T. Tokioka, A.J. Weaver, and T.M.L. Wigley, 1996: Climate models—projections of future climate. *In*: Climate Change 1995: The Science of Climate Change. Contribution of Working Group I to the Second Assessment Report of the Intergovernmental Panel on Climate Change [Houghton, J.T., L.G. Meira Filho, B. A. Callander, N. Harris, A. Kattenberg, and K. Maskell *(eds.)*]. Cambridge University Press; Cambridge, United Kingdom and New York, NY, USA, pp. 289-357.

Kilbourne, E.M., 1989. Heatwaves. *In*: The Public Health Consequences of Disasters [Gregg, M.B. *(ed.)*]. U.S. Department of Health and Human Services, Public Health Service, Centers for Disease Control and Prevention, Atlanta, GA, USA, pp. 51-61.

Kleidon, A., Heimann, M. 1999. Deep-rooted vegetation, Amazonian deforestation, and climate: results from a modelling study. Global Ecology and Biogeography 8: 397-405.

Kovats, R.S., M.J. Bouma, and A. Haines. 1999. EI Niño and Health. WHO/SDE/PHE/99.4, World Health Organization, Geneva, Switzerland, 48 pp.

Lake, P.S. Palmer, M.A., Biro, P., Cole, J., Covich, A.P., Dahm, C.; Gibert, J., Goedkoop, W., Martens, K., Verhoeven, J. 2000. Global change and the biodiversity of freshwater ecosystems: impacts on linkages between above-sediment and sediment biota. BioScience 50(12): 1099-1107.

Latini, A.O. and Petrere Jr, M. 2004. Reduction of a native fish fauna by alien species: an example from Brazilian freshwater tropical lakes: Fisheries Management and Ecology 11(2): 71-79.

Laurance, W.F., and G.B. Williamson. 2001. Positive feedbacks among forest fragmentation, drought, and climate change in the Amazon. Conservation Biology 15(6): 1529-1535.

Laurance, W.F., G.B. Williamson, P. Delamonica, A. Oliveira, T.E. Lovejoy, C. Gascon, and L. Pohl. 2001. Effects of a strong drought on Amazonian forest fragments and edges. Journal of Tropical Ecology 17: 771-785.

McClain, M.E. 2001. The Relevance of Biogeochemistry to Amazon Development and Conservation. In The biogeochemistry of the Amazon Basin. McClain, M.E., Victoria, R.L., and Richey, J.E. (eds.). London, Oxford University Press.

Marengo, J., U. Bhatt, and C. Cunningham, 2000: Decadal and multidecadal variability of climate in the Amazon basin. *International Journal of Climatolology.*

Marengo, J., Tomasella, J., and Uvo, C. R.: 1998. Trends in Streamflow and Rainfall in Tropical South America: Amazonia, Eastern Brazil, and Northwestern Peru. Journal of Geophysical Research 103: 1775-1783.

Markham, A. (*ed*). 1998. Potential impacts of climate change on tropical forest ecosystems. Kluwer Academic Publishers, Dordrecht, The Netherlands.

Martens, W.J.M. 1998. Climate change, thermal stress and mortality changes. Social Science and Medicine, 46(3): 331-344.

Martinez, J.O., J.L. González, O.H. Pilkey, and W.J. Neal. 1995. Tropical barrier islands of Colombia Pacific coast: sixty-two barrier islands. Journal of Coastal Research 11(2): 432-453.

McMichael, A.J., M. Ando, R. Carcavallo, P. Epstein, A. Haines, G. Jendritzky, L. Kalkstein, R. Odongo, J. Patz, and W. Piver. 1996. Human population health. *In*: Climate Change 1995: Impacts, Adaptations, and Mitigation of Climate Change. Contribution of Working Group II to the Second Assessment Report of the Intergovernmental Panel on Climate Change [Watson, R.T., MC. Zinyowera, and R.H. Moss (*eds.*)]. Cambridge University Press, Cambridge, United Kingdom and New York, NY, USA, pp. 561-584.

Miles, L. A. Grainger, Phillips, O. 2004. The impact of global climate change on tropical biodiversity in Amazonia. Global Ecology and Biogeography 13: 553-565.

Mitchell, J.F.B., R.A. Davis, W.J. Ingram, and C.A. Senior, 1995. On surface temperature, greenhouse gases and aerosols: models and observations. Journal of Climate 10: 2364-2386.

Moreira, C.J.E. 1986. Rainfall and flooding in the Guayas river basin and its effects on the incidence of malaria 1982-1985. Disasters 10(2): 107-111.

National Institute for Space Research (INPE). 2005. Figures obtained from the National Institute for Space Research website, www.inpe.br, cited August 29, 2005.

Nepstad, D., G. Carvalho, A.C. Barros, A. Alencar, J.P. Capobianco, J. Bishop, P. Moutinho, P. Lefebvre, U. Lopes Silva Jr., E. Prins. 2001. Road paving, fire regime feedbacks, and the future of Amazon forests. Forest Ecology and Management 154 (3): 395-407.

Nijssen, B. O'Donnell, G.M., Hamlet, A.F. and Lettenmaier, D.P. 2001. Hydrologic Sensitivity of Global Rivers to Climate Change. 50(1-2): 143-175.

OPS, 1998. Repercusiones Sanitaria de la Oscilacióndel Sur(El Nino). CE122/10, Organización Panamericana de la Salud, Washington, DC, USA, 22 pp. (in Spanish).

Pabón, J.D., 1995a. Búsqueda de series de referencia para el seguimiento de la señal regional del calentamiento global. *Cuadernos de Gegrofla,* 2, 164-173 (in Spanish).

Pabón, J.D., G.E. León, E.S. Rangel, J.E. Montealegre, G. Hurtado, and J.A. Zea, I999b. *El Cambio Climático en Colombia: Tendencias actuates y Proyecciones.* Nota Técnica del IDEAM, IDEAM/METEO/002-99, Santa Fe de Bogotá, Colombia, 20 pp. (in Spanish).

PAHO, 1998a. Report on the Epidemiological Situation in Central America. SC/XVII/40, Pan American Health Organization, Washington, DC, USA, 2 pp.

PAHO, 1998b. Infectious Diseases Posing in the Greatest Epidemiological Risk Following Hurricane Mitch in Central America, 1998. A Report of the Pan American Health Organization Emergency Task Force, Division of Disease Prevention and Control, Washington, DC, USA, 4 pp.

Patz, J.A., W.J.M. Martens, D.A. Focks, and T.H. Jetten, 1998. Dengue fever epidemic potential as projected by general circulation models of global climate change. Environmental Health Perspectives 106(3): 147-153.

Pitcher, T. J, Hart, P. J. B. 1982. Fisheries Ecology. London: Croom Helm.

Rao, V. B., Satyarmurty, P., and Brito, J. I. B. 1986. On the 1983 drought in Northeast Brazil. Journal of Climate 6: 43-51.

Reilly, J. W. Baethgen, F.E. Chege, S.C. van de Geijn, L. Erda, A. Iglesias, G. Kenny, D. Patterson, J. Rogasik, R. Rotter, C. Rosenzweig. W. Sombroek, J. Westbrook, D. Bachelet; M. Brklacich, U. Dammgen, M. Howden, R.J.V. Joyce, P.D. Lingren, D. Schimmelpfennig. U. Singh, O. Sirotenko, and E. Wheaton. 1996. Agriculture in a changing climate: impacts and adaptation. *In*: Climate Change 1995: Impacts, Adaptations and Mitigation of Climate Change: Scientific-Technical Analyses. Contribution of Working Group II to the Second Assessment Report of the Intergovernmental Panel on Climate Change [Watson, R.T., M.C. Zinyowera, and R.H. Moss (*eds.*)]. Cambridge University Press, Cambridge, United Kingdom and New York, NY, USA, pp. 427-467.

Rosas, I., G. Roy-Ocotla, and P. Mosiño, 1989. Meteorological effects on variation of airborne algae in Mexico. International Journal of Biometeorology 33: 173-179.

Rosenfeld, D. 1999. TRMM observed first direct evidence of smoke from forest fires inhibiting rainfall. Geophysical Research Letters 26 (20): 3105-3108.

Rosenzweig, C. and D. Hillel, 1998. Climate Change and the Global Harvest: Potential Impacts of the Greenhouse Effect on Agriculture. Oxford University Press, Oxford. United Kingdom, 324 pp.

Rosenzweig, C, M.L. Parry, G. Fischer, and K. Frohberg. 1993. Climate Change and World Food Supply. Research Report

No. 3, Environmental Change Unit. Oxford University, Oxford, United Kingdom, 28 pp.

Salati, E., and P. B. Vose. 1984. Amazon basin: A system in equilibrium. Science 225: 129-138.

Shukla, J., Nobre, C., and Sellers, P. 1990. Amazon deforestation and climate change. Science 247: 1322-1325.

Solomon, A.M., I.C. Prentice, R. Leemann, and W. P. Cramer. 1993. The interaction of climate and land use in future terrestrial carbon storage and release. Water, Air, and Soil Pollution 70: 595–614.

Tian, H.Q., J.M. Melillo, D.W. Kicklighter, A D. McGuire, J.V.K. Helfrich, B. Moore, and CJ. Vorosmarty. 1998. Effect of interannual climate variability on carbon storage in Amazonian ecosystems. Nature 396 (6712): 664-667.

Quintana-Gomez, R.A., 1999: Trends of maximum and minimum temperatures in northern South America. Journal of Climate, 12(7), 2104-2112.

Victoria, R., L. Marinelli, J. Moraes, M. Ballester, A. Krusche, G. Pellegrino, R. Almeida, and J. Richey, 1998: Surface air temperature variations in the Amazon region and its border during this century. Journal of Climate, 11, 1105-1110.

Wara, M.W., Ravelo, A.C., Delaney: M.L. 2005. Permanent EI Niño-Like Conditions During the Pliocene Warm Period. Science, 309 (5735): 758-761.

Welcomme R.L. 1985. River fisheries. Food and Agriculture Organisation Fisheries Technical Paper 262, 330.

White, A., M.G.R. Cannel, and A.D. Friend. 1999. Climate change impacts on ecosystems and the terrestrial carbon sink: a new assessment. Global Environmental Change, 9, S 21-S 30.

World Meteorological Organisation WMO, 1998: Report on the Status of Observing Networks. Report submitted to CoP-4, World Meteorological Organisation, Geneva, Switzerland.

Wooton, R.J. 1990. Ecology of Teleost Fishes. New York: Chapman & Hall.

Zuidema, G., G.J. Van den Born, J. Alcamo, and G.J.J. Kreileman, 1994. Simulating changes in global land cover as affected by economic and climatic factors. Water, Air, and Soil Pollution 76 (1-2): 163-198.

Canada's Inuit Peoples Are Affected by Arctic Melting

Emily Gertz

In 2004, the Arctic Climate Impact Assessment shared with the world its findings that the Arctic is experiencing the most rapid and extreme climate change on Earth. The Inuit, the Arctic's native people, claim to have noticed changes in ice, water, land, and wildlife years before the assessment was released. These changes in the environment have led the Inuit to try and preserve their culture by working to link climate change with human rights in order to file a possible lawsuit in U.S. federal courts. Emily Gertz is a journalist and editor specializing in the environment, technology, and science.

As you read, consider the following questions:

1. What are two animals the Inuit have traditionally relied on for sustenance?
2. What species of animals did native Intuits observe changes in?
3. How are chemicals and pollutants like chlordane, DDT, and PCBs accumulated in the Artic?

When Sheila Watt-Cloutier was growing up in Kuujjuaq, an Inuit village in far northern Quebec, summer days never got hot enough for shorts and T-shirts. Only the very

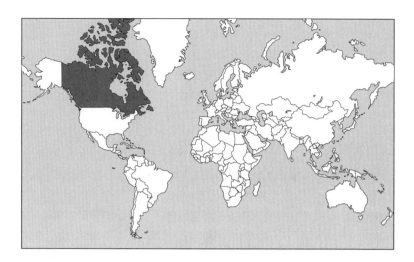

brave ventured into the frigid local river for a swim. But now, she says, there are many warm days, and "the whole community goes down and spends days beaching it and trying to cool themselves off."

Needless to say, a day at the beach is not a normal Arctic activity. The climate shifts responsible for that change are also melting ice sheets, eroding the region's coastlines, and shrinking habitat for polar bears, caribou, and other animals the Inuit have long relied on for sustenance. While other citizens of the world debate the very existence of climate change, the Arctic is melting—and the mainstays of this indigenous northern culture are disappearing with it.

Robins and barn owls—birds for which the Inuit had no name—appeared for the first time.

Watt-Cloutier refuses to stand by while that happens. The 51-year-old is the elected chair of the Inuit Circumpolar Conference [ICC], a federation of Native nations representing about 150,000 people in Canada, Greenland, Russia, and the U.S. To save their homes, their prey, and themselves, the ICC is taking on the world's largest, most recalcitrant greenhouse-gas emitter, the country the Inuit say is driving them extinct: the United States of America. The group is, as Watt-Cloutier puts it, "defending our right to be cold."

You Say You Want a Resolution

Last November, the multinational Arctic Climate Impact Assessment startled the world with its findings that the Arctic was experiencing "some of the most rapid and severe climate change on Earth." The international press was awash with stories about the ice cap vanishing and polar bears going extinct, as well as Bush administration attempts to derail the report's policy recommendations.

But the findings were hardly news to the Inuit. In fact, two years earlier, the ICC had begun investigating how to get industrialized nations—in particular, the U.S.—to act on global warming. They'd consulted environmental lawyers Martin Wagner and Don Goldberg, who were already working together to link climate change to human rights. The pair advised ICC that filing a petition with the Inter-American Commission on Human Rights might be the way to go. The commission, part of the Organization of American States, has no power of enforcement, but a finding in favor of the Inuit could be the basis for future lawsuits in U.S. federal courts.

"The impacts of climate change have very real, negative, harmful impacts on the Inuits' ability to sustain themselves as they have traditionally done, their ability to be healthy, which they have a right to in the Inter-American human-rights system," explains Wagner, of Earthjustice. "Their ability to maintain their unique culture, which is absolutely dependent on ice and snow; their ability to hunt and fish and harvest plant foods; their ability to have shelter and build their homes—all of those rights are impacted by climate change in the Arctic."

The Inuit had been noticing alterations in ice, land, water, and wildlife for years—phenomena that fell outside their extensive traditional knowledge. Ice formed later in the year and broke up sooner. Changes in the ice pack altered travel routes over land and sea. Experienced hunters were falling through thinning ice into seawater cold enough to kill in minutes. Once-frozen coastlines were eroding, destroying Inuit homes.

Also potentially devastating, residents were observing changes in the creatures around them, including caribou, polar bears, ringed seals, walrus, beluga whales, and seabirds. The culture has relied on these animals for food, clothing, and other materials for thousands of years. Now, increasingly, they were noticing that polar bears couldn't find seals along the receding ice edge and were forced to scavenge elsewhere for food. A mosquito invasion drove caribou into the hills during the summer, forcing them to forsake rich lowland grazing for scrappier fare. And robins and barn owls—birds for which the Inuit had no name—appeared for the first time.

Anxious to protect life as they know it, the ICC floated a trial balloon about the human-rights petition in December 2003, at the ninth annual meeting of nations and nongovernmental organizations negotiating the Kyoto Protocol. For years, these meetings had been dominated by relatively arcane discussions on science and policy. Resistance to the treaty—at that point both Russia and the United States were refusing to sign, effectively hog-tying the entire agreement—had left many negotiators and activists dispirited. But the reaction to the ICC's presentation was electric.

"It resonated truth for people," Watt-Cloutier says. "And it gave a sense of energy into this process, because then it was people-oriented. It was human." Encouraged by the response, the ICC and its lawyers continued to develop their case, and announced at last year's [2004] Kyoto negotiations in Buenos Aires that they'd be going forward.

Once the petition is filed, possibly by the end of this year [2005], it could take two years or more for the commission to make a determination. (Last year, 1,349 complaints were filed with the commission, 57 involving the U.S.) But Goldberg,

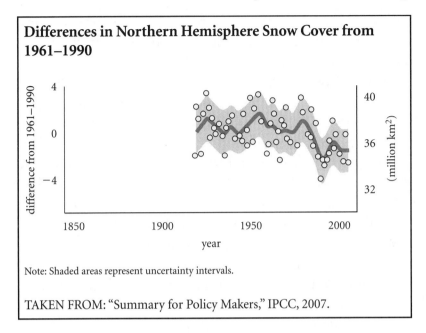

Differences in Northern Hemisphere Snow Cover from 1961–1990

Note: Shaded areas represent uncertainty intervals.

TAKEN FROM: "Summary for Policy Makers," IPCC, 2007.

who works for the Center for International Environmental Law, feels the ICC's move has already made an impact. "I think the thing it's done most dramatically is end the debate that this is a problem that's somewhere out there in the future," he says. "When you're talking about . . . entire villages being forced to relocate . . . and buildings and telephone poles falling over, I think that hits people on a different level. It is very visceral."

Culture Clubbed

Global warming is not the first industrial threat to reach this land. In the late 1980s, medical research revealed that chemicals and pollutants including chlordane, DDT, and PCBs, had been accumulating in the globe's farthest north for decades, carried from thousands of miles away by atmospheric and oceanic currents—or, as scientists have more recently supposed, by bird droppings. These persistent organic pollutants, or POPs, become more concentrated higher in the food chain, reaching unprecedented levels in predator mammals at the top like polar bears, ringed seals, beluga whales, walrus—and Inuit, who carry more than 200 toxic pollutants in their bodies.

This poisoning from afar means "we have to think twice about how we deal with going out into the environment," says Watt-Cloutier, "because the environment's our supermarket, it's our way of getting food back to our families and to our communities." Canadian Inuit mothers, for example, who have seven times more PCBs [pollutants] in their breast milk than women in the country's largest cities, are advised either not to nurse their babies, or not to eat meat from the hunt.

The ICC was involved in years of international negotiations on POPs, culminating in last year's ratification of the Stockholm Convention, which banned 12 chemicals termed the "Dirty Dozen." The group is now active in the agreement's implementation.

The Inuit have also struggled to survive a cultural dissolution common to many indigenous peoples who have experienced rapid modernization. Canadian Inuit struggle with some of the highest rates of alcoholism and drug abuse in the nation. Inuit infant mortality rates are two to three times higher than the Canadian national average, life expectancy is about five to seven years shorter, and the suicide rate is six times higher.

Watt-Cloutier says the solutions to these challenges lie, quite literally, on the ice. "The actual act of going out on the land, and the skills that are required to survive these conditions that we have in the Arctic, are the very skills . . . young people need to survive even the modern world," she says. "What the land teaches you . . . is to be bold under pressure, to withstand stress, to be courageous, to be patient, to have sound judgment, and ultimately wisdom."

"Everything is connected," she continues. "Connectivity is going to be the key to addressing these issues, like contaminants and climate change. They're not just about contaminants on your plate. They're not just about the ice depleting. They're about the issue of humanity. What we do every day—whether you live in Mexico, the United States, Russia, China . . . can have a very negative impact on an entire way of life for an entire people far away from that source."

. . . her [Watt-Cloutier's] grandmother often told her how citizens of the southern nation saved many Inuit from starvation during the Second World War, when the U.S. military used the Arctic as a base for some operations.

A Whole New World?

While human rights have usually been considered in local contexts—violations of a person's rights by fellow citizens or one's own government—the Inuit petition to the Inter-American Commission makes connections in a global context, arguing that the actions of one nation can violate the rights of people beyond its own borders. Goldberg and Wagner feel the case has the potential to transform the entire politics of global warming.

The petition is unique, says Wagner, "in that it's making this connection between climate change and human rights. It's unique because it's raising an environmental claim against the United States. It's asking the commission to recognize the international obligation of the United States for its failure to take action to protect the environment, and to recognize the implications of U.S. inaction for people both [inside and outside] the United States."

That request isn't sitting well with some. According to Goldberg, representatives from groups known for disputing global warming science—including the Washington, D.C.-based, right-wing think tank the Competitive Enterprise Institute—showed up at the ICC presentation in Buenos Aires last year, asking pointed and misleading questions. "[They] were not just questioning, but were being very argumentative," he says. The ICC also found some of its posters and fliers around the conference grounds ripped down, or slashed through with red arrows pointing at a flier denouncing the Arctic Climate Impact Assessment as "junk science."

"I have to say, I detected a note of desperation," says Goldberg. "These negotiations have always maintained a level of seriousness that I thought was really violated by these kinds of activities." . . .

This summer, Wagner, Goldberg, and the ICC will continue gathering facts to support their case, including videotaped testimony by Inuit elders. In the meantime, Watt-Cloutier's stature as a global activist is growing: in April, she accepted a U.N. Champions of the Earth award and helped stage a massive, Hollywood-infused "Global Warming" photo shoot on the ice in Nunavut, Canada's Inuit territory; in June, she generated headlines from Norway when she accepted the International Sophie Prize, given annually to a recipient "working toward a sustainable future."

She has also met with two consuls at the U.S. Consulate General in Quebec City in recent years, and testified at a hearing on climate-change policy organized by Sen. John McCain (R-Ariz.) last September. "I am very open to talking to anyone in the State Department, or anybody else, who would like to sit down and dialogue about these issues," she says. "I am still hoping that the United States will be able to start to change their views about how they do this." The U.S. has not yet offered an official response to the announcement of the pending petition.

Watt-Cloutier is careful to stress that there's no history of antagonism between the Inuit and the United States; in fact, her grandmother often told her how citizens of the southern nation saved many Inuit from starvation during the Second World War, when the U.S. military used the Arctic as a base for some operations.

"I am trying to bring back that sense of connectivity, and understanding, and responsibility," Watt-Cloutier says. The human-rights appeal, she says, "is defending a way of life for ourselves. But it becomes the Inuit path in the human journey."

Italy's Canal City of Venice Must Cope with Rising Sea Levels

Eric Jaffe

The Italian government has recently put billions of dollars into developing a barrier to protect the city from the rising tide. This complex system of floodgates known as MOSE was started in 2003 and is scheduled to be completed by 2012. MOSE has drawn severe criticism from Italian citizens due to its expensive $4.5 billion price tag; however, something is necessary to combat the rising tide. Eric Jaffe is a writer for Smithsonian Magazine, *a monthly magazine chronicling the arts, history, sciences and popular culture of the times.*

As you read, consider the following questions:

1. If the tide in Venice rises to 43 inches, how much of the city will be covered in shallow water?

2. How will the MOSE system work to protect Venice from seawater?

3. What percentage of water samples in Venice tested positive for disease-causing agents?

Fabio Carrera has been studying the Venice lagoon since 1988, so when he heard a high tide siren one evening in 2002, it wasn't the first time. But it might have been the strangest.

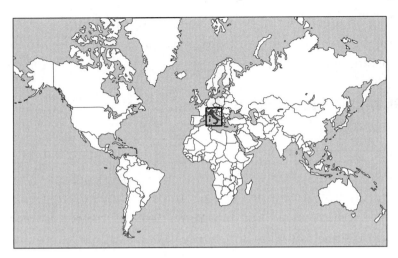

The sirens warn Venetians that the tide has reached roughly 43 inches—enough to spread shallow water across 12 percent of the city. These alarms typically sound in fall or winter. But here stood Carrera in early June and the tide had reached more than 47 inches, the only summer tide above 43 since modern records began in 1923.

To Carrera, a Venice native and urban information scientist at Worcester Polytechnic Institute in Massachusetts, the event was an early symptom of the impact climate change is having on sea levels in Venice. "Things seem to be off," he says. "Things like a weird summer high tide—those are the best indicators that something's happening in the lagoon."

Venice lacks modern sewage, relying instead on tides to flush wastes from the canals into the Adriatic Sea.

Flooding in Venice is nothing new. High tides have been invading the city since the 6th century. The biggest tide on record hit November 4, 1966, reaching more than six feet above sea level. In the decades that followed, the Italian government poured billions into developing a barrier, finally settling on a complex system of floodgates, called MOSE. Building began in 2003 and the system is scheduled to be operational by 2012.

Is MOSE the Solution Venice Is Looking For?

But recent global warming forecasts have caused MOSE—already controversial for its $4.5 billion price tag—to draw scrutiny from scientists the way St. Mark's Square draws tourists. A report issued this February [2007] by the Intergovernmental Panel on Climate Change [IPCC] calls into question whether the elaborate floodgate will be sufficient to handle changing sea levels.

The report predicts a rise between about seven inches and two feet within the next 100 years. That range could increase by another seven inches or more based on ice sheet melting in Greenland and Antarctica. MOSE will only protect the city from a sea level increase of about two feet, says Pierpaolo Campostrini, director of CORILA, which organizes all scientific research in Venice.

"It's not changing anything," says Campostrini of the new report. "It's just confirming our worries."

The barriers rest at the three inlets where the Adriatic Sea feeds into the lagoon. When a high tide looms, air will pump up the MOSE system, blocking the sea water from spilling into the city. Even if global warming does eventually push MOSE's limits, Campostrini says, the floodgates will buy scientists several decades of time to figure out a long-term solution. Meanwhile, as sea level rise approaches two feet, the barriers might simply spend more time closed.

This stall tactic could come at a high price, explains biologist Richard Gersberg of San Diego State University. Closing the barriers could complicate the city's precarious sewage situ-

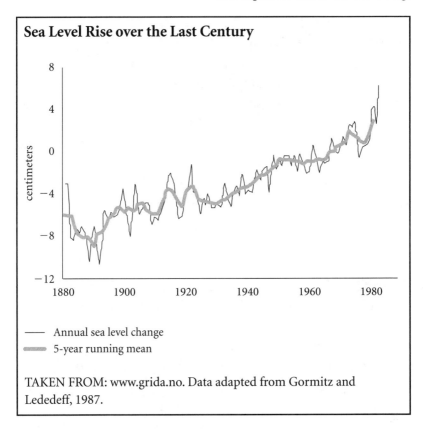

Sea Level Rise over the Last Century

— Annual sea level change

▬ 5-year running mean

TAKEN FROM: www.grida.no. Data adapted from Gormitz and Lededeff, 1987.

ation and cause health problems. Venice lacks modern sewage, relying instead on tides to flush wastes from the canals into the Adriatic Sea.

Venice's Sewage Problem

"There's a concern that, when the barriers come up, then that flushing will be cut off," says Gersberg. "MOSE gates, from what I've read, are supposed to be closed for only a short time. But is sea level going to cooperate with that theory? My best guess is, no."

Gersberg and his colleagues recently conducted a three-year study of the water quality in the canals that make up the Venice lagoon, and at a beach of nearby Lido. Almost 80 percent of the samples analyzed from nine sites in the lagoon tested positive for two types of disease-causing agents, Gersberg's team reports in the July 2006 *Water Research*.

The findings are not yet a cause for alarm, says Gersberg. At Lido, where tourists are allowed to swim, the pathogen levels were much lower and met European health standards. Those who stick to the city will be safe with only minimal precautions—not dipping their hands in the lagoon from the side of a gondola, for example.

The situation would likely worsen over time, though, if MOSE's gates remained closed for long periods. "Taking sewage when it floods and having people walk around in it—to not expect a health problem, you would have to be an eternal optimist," Gersberg says.

So far, and somewhat ironically, climate change's biggest impact on Venice has been that sea level forecasts might have spurred the government to move ahead with MOSE after years of sitting on the plans. Construction is 30 percent complete, says Campostrini, and few other options exist. In one scenario still being investigated, officials would pump water below the city surface, raising it as much as a foot.

Filmmakers Marylou and Jerome Bongiorno recently gathered several scientists, including Carrera, to discuss MOSE and alternative defenses against rising sea levels, as part of their research for a documentary and feature film focusing on climate change in Venice. The problems, they say, are not as far away as they seem.

"You have to look at Venice and say, 'It's already happening,'" says Marylou, whose parents are native Venetians. "'Global warming' has become this fashionable term, but we don't want everybody to say, 'It's going to be hot this summer,' and think that's global warming."

The researchers kicked around several ideas, says Jerome, from planting boats in various regions of the lagoon that would divert incoming sea water, to building a wall around the entire city.

"At a certain point, MOSE is not going to work anymore," he says. "Why not build a pretty wall now that becomes part of the city's culture?"

To satisfy Gersberg's fears, building a "Great Wall of Venice" would require retrofitting the city's classic buildings with modern sewage—a daunting task. Such an enclosure could still impact marine life and create economic problems by cutting off access to shipping harbors. Not to mention the facelift it would give a city known to value tradition. An attraction of MOSE, says Campostrini, is that it preserves the current look of the lagoon.

The Future of Venice

Lagoon or not, Venice might cease being operational without a more drastic plan, says Carrera. Though MOSE will do some good, he says, it's a bit like building a dome around Boston to keep away occasional snowstorms: A passable solution, yes. But probably not the best use of resources.

"If global warming's worst predictions come true in 100 years," says Carrera, "the real issue is preserving Venice as a liveable place—not stopping the occasional tide from coming in."

Periodical Bibliography

The following articles have been selected to supplement the diverse views presented in this chapter.

Steve Connor — "Impact of Climate Change 'Can Be Likened to WMD,'" *The Independent*, November 29, 2005.

Douglas Fischer — "Global Warming Impacts Aren't Waiting for Future," *Oakland Tribune*, May 24, 2007.

Todd Hartman — "Climate Report Cites Risks for Colorado," *Rocky Mountain News*, April 7, 2007.

H. Josef Hebert — "Climate Change May Impact Health," *Deseret News*, April 10, 2008.

William P. Hoar — "Truth Melts Down," *The New American*, December 13, 2004.

Anna McAninch — "Potential Impacts of Climate Change on Tropical Forest Ecosystems," *Northeastern Naturalist*, January 1, 1999.

Mongabay.com — "Global Warming Puts Primates at Greater Risk," October 25, 2007, www.mongabay.com.

Virginia Morell — "Signs from Earth: Now What?" *National Geographic*, September 2004.

Jim Motavalli — "SOS for Reefs—The Impact of Global Warming on Coral Reefs," *E: The Environmental Magazine*, November 1, 1999.

Matt Nisbett — "Alternative Medicine, Impact Threats, Abrupt Climate Change, and Efficient Energy," *Skeptical Inquirer*, November 11, 1998.

Sean Ryan — "Building Industry Has Significant Impact on Global Warming," *The Daily Reporter* (Milwaukee), April 23, 2007.

ScienceDaily.com — "Climate Change Could Impact Vital Functions of Microbes," 2008. www.sciencedaily.com.

GLOBALVIEWPOINTS

CHAPTER 3

Developing Nations and Climate Change

Climate Change Disproportionately Affects the Inhabitants of Developing Nations

Rachel Oliver

Rachel Oliver asserts that climate change will disproportionately affect the world's poorest citizens. Citing research from the United Nations and international aid organizations, Oliver explores how the world's least developed regions are the most susceptible to environmental degradation. This degradation is exacerbated by the world's largest consumers and heaviest polluters—mostly citizens and companies in the wealthiest nations. Rachel Oliver is a reporter and project coordinator for CNN's online media.

As you read, consider the following questions:

1. How much money does roughly half the world's population survive on per day?
2. One-sixth of the world's population will face what because of retreating glaciers?
3. Stephen Pacala, director of the Princeton Environmental Institute, claimed that the world's 500 million richest people were responsible for what percentage of all greenhouse gas emissions?

The general dialogue on adapting to a world affected by climate change by definition excludes the world's poorest people. And yet it's the world's poorest who are often put forward as the ones who are likely to feel the affects of climate change the most and are likely to be able to deal with them the least.

Around half of the world's population—slightly fewer than 3 billion people—survives on less than $2 a day. None of them are likely to go shopping for an automobile any time soon in a bid to reduce on their greenhouse gas emissions; and investing in photo voltaic solar panels to put on their rooftops probably won't be a priority, either.

Comparing the average annual per capita carbon footprints of the rich and poor certainly makes for unsettling reading: The average American's annual carbon footprint—20.4 tons—is around 2,000 times that of someone living in the African nation of Chad. And the average Briton will emit as much carbon dioxide (CO_2) in one day as a Kenyan will in an entire year.

Between 1990 and 1998, more than 94 percent of the world's biggest natural disasters (and there were 568 of them) occurred in the developing world.

Overall, the United Nations estimates that the carbon footprint of the world's 1 billion poorest people (those living on less than $1 a day) represents just 3 percent of the global total.

By contrast, if you look at the cumulative buildup of carbon dioxide (CO_2) in the atmosphere since the Industrial Revolution, then the responsibility for a whopping 80 percent of the world's emissions lies with just 20 percent of the inhabitants of the world's wealthiest nations (at the time this figure was calculated it only included Europe, North America and the former Soviet Union).

Developing World Braced for Disaster

Between 1990 and 1998, more than 94 percent of the world's biggest natural disasters (and there were 568 of them) occurred in the developing world, according to Oxfam. One of the reasons is that 75 percent of the world's poor live in rural areas, relying on the land to make a living. These people, says the World Resources Institute (WRI), are "disproportionately affected by environmental degradation."

Poverty-stricken people in the developing world face an uncertain future. Just some of their chief concerns include:

- One-sixth of the world's population will face water shortages because of retreating glaciers

- 1 billion of the poorest people on Earth will lose their livelihoods to desertification

- More than 200 million environmental refugees will be created by 2050, as a direct result of rising sea levels, erosion and agricultural damage

- Around 17 million Bangladeshis could find themselves without homes by 2030 due to flooding, cyclones and tornadoes

- More than 60 million more Africans will be exposed to Malaria if temperatures rise by 2 degrees Celsius

- 182 million Sub-Saharan Africans could die of disease "directly attributable" to climate change by the end of the century

- In Asia, the homes of 94 million people could be flooded by the end of the century

It's People, Not Nations

More people are beginning to refer to this phenomenon as "environmental injustice," and it has rankled those who see climate change as a "rich nations' problem." This has led one ecological economist, professor Richard Norgaard from the University of California [UC]-Berkeley, to claim that the world's rich countries owe the world's poor $2.3 trillion—an amount that easily eclipses the total of Third World debt ($1.8 trillion).

That figure represents the ecological damage caused by the consumption of goods. The UC-Berkeley researchers have called the figure "conservative," since it only accounts for greenhouse gas emissions, ozone layer depletion, agriculture, deforestation, over fishing and converting mangrove swamps. It doesn't account for damage caused by war, loss of biodiversity or freshwater withdrawals, for example.

But climate change won't just be punishing for those in the developing world: More studies are showing that if you are poor anywhere in the world, you are more at risk from the various hazards environmental degradation poses than your more affluent peers.

According to UNEP [United Nations Environment Programme], in Los Angeles more than 71 percent of African-Americans live in "highly polluted areas," compared to 24 percent of whites. Across the United States, black children are three times more likely to have "hazardous levels of lead in their blood" as a result of living near hazardous waste sites.

There are costs involved with climate change, too—higher fuel and food bills in particular. An independent study last year in the UK [United Kingdom] showed that the number of households being forced to decide between food and heating has almost doubled in just two years. This, over a period when electricity prices jumped by 39 percent and gas prices by 61 percent.

So is there a link between environmental injustices and the disparities in consumption levels? Does the former in fact reflect the latter to some degree? More people are beginning to believe that the burden of climate change rests with affluent individuals, not wealthy nations.

A recent study in Australia found that wealthy, tertiary-educated citizens produced more than twice as many greenhouse gas emissions—around 58 tons per capita per year—than that nation's low-income families, which on average produced 22 tons a year. The calculations, made by the National Institute of Economic and Industry Research, were based on consumption levels.

Authors J. Timmons Roberts and Bradley C. Parks suggest the same point. In their book, *A Climate of Injustice: Global Inequality, North-South Politics, and Climate Policy*, Roberts and Parks point to a 1996 study that showed that people in the United States who earned more than $75,000 emitted nearly four times as much CO_2 as those who earned less than $10,000.

Comparing disparities between nations was difficult, the authors said, but yet they made one definitive declaration:

"It can be said with confidence that the world's richest people cause emissions thousands of times greater than those of the world's poorest."

Emissions Trail Leads to Small Group of People

While previous studies have put the majority of the greenhouse gas tally on the shoulders of 20 percent of the world's richest, Stephen Pacala, the director of the Princeton Environmental Institute, said an even smaller group may be responsible.

Speaking last year, Pacala said a disproportionate responsibility could lie with as few as 7 percent of us. The world's 500 million richest people were responsible for a breathtaking 50 percent of all greenhouse gas emissions, he claimed.

He is calling for a "new rhetoric of fairness" in the fight against climate change. Put simply, if you want to tackle emissions, Pacala says, stop targeting countries and start targeting people—because the world's biggest emitters don't all live in

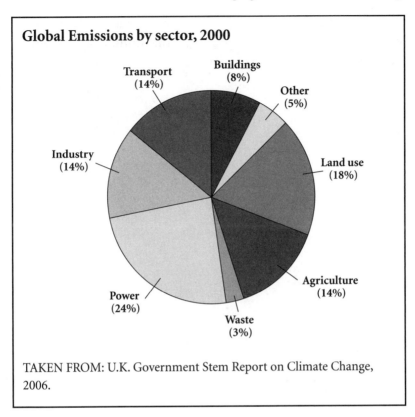

Global Emissions by sector, 2000

- Transport (14%)
- Buildings (8%)
- Other (5%)
- Land use (18%)
- Agriculture (14%)
- Waste (3%)
- Power (24%)
- Industry (14%)

TAKEN FROM: U.K. Government Stem Report on Climate Change, 2006.

one place (India is presently producing more new millionaires each year than any other country, for example, and is viewed as the biggest wealth creator in the world, according to Boston Consulting Group).

"The responsibility for emissions reductions does not travel with national identity," Pacala said. "It travels with your emissions, and your emissions go hand-in-hand with your income."

The Sierra Club divides the world's population into three different classes representing different percentages of the world's population: the poor (20 percent), the middle class (60 percent) and the "consumer class" (20 percent). It squarely blames consumption for ecological destruction and points the finger at the "consumer class" for making this so.

The group's real concern, however, is what happens to the 60 percent of people that reside in the middle who want to move up into the next category.

Poor Nations Must Also Work to Cut Carbon Emissions

Haider Rizvi

Haider Rizvi reports on scientific research on greenhouse gas emissions from developing nations. The study found that rising emissions from developing nations would still significantly contribute to climate change even if the world's most developed nations produced no emissions. Rizvi asserts that the world's developing nations, mostly located in the global south, must balance fostering growth with reducing emissions. Haider Rizvi is an international contributor to OneWorld.net and Common Dreams, a progressive online news source.

As you read, consider the following questions:

1. On what premise was the Kyoto Protocol based?
2. Where are the world's two largest carbon dioxide emitting power plants located?
3. What is the threshold that the Intergovernmental Panel on Climate Change (IPCC) links with large irreversible climatic impacts?

Rising carbon emissions from developing countries would threaten the world with severe climate change within a single generation, even if rich countries were to stop their

Haider Rizvi, "Poor Countries Must Also Curtail Carbon Emissions," December 6, 2007. www.us.oneworld.net. Copyright © 2007 The OneWorld.net. Reprinted by permission of OneWorld US. OneWorld.net is an online hub for people who care about the world beyond their own borders.

own greenhouse gas emissions tomorrow, according to a new study by an independent think tank.

The study's findings challenge the notion that the rich countries mainly responsible for carbon emissions can tackle the problem of global warming by themselves, and that as a result, poor countries can develop along a carbon-intensive path until they are much richer.

The new research by the Washington, D.C.-based Center for Global Development (CGD) shows that fossil-fueled growth in emerging economies could lead to a climate crisis long before incomes reach rich-country levels.

The study's authors say their findings may have important implications for the United Nations' annual climate change conference being held this week [December 2007] in Bali [Indonesia].

At [the United Nations Conference on Climate Change in] Bali, top policy makers from about 130 nations are working towards a new pact to cut greenhouse-gas emissions—one that goes well beyond the Kyoto Protocol.

The Kyoto Protocol, developed in the mid-1990s, is based on the premise that highly industrialized countries of the North should rapidly cut their emissions, while developing countries in the South can continue to pursue industrialization to meet social and development needs.

The finding that the South is on its way to creating its own global warming crisis "should not be seen as a cause for complacency in the rich countries, or as somehow absolving us from taking action." . . .

Cutting Greenhouse Emissions in the Global South

"But from the perspective of the South's own self-interest, focusing exclusively on the Northern sources of this problem is a dangerous distraction," says David Wheeler, the lead author of the new study, and the head of CGD's Confronting Climate Change initiative.

"The question," according to Wheeler, "is not whether or not the South will commit to emissions reductions—under any scenario it eventually must for its own sake. But, will it do so in time?"

The study, entitled "Another Inconvenient Truth: A Carbon-Intensive South Faces Environmental Disaster, No Matter What the North Does," predicts significant costs to cutting emissions, which, according to researchers, "must be shared without taking away from poverty reduction."

Wheeler and the study's co-author, Kevin Ummel, compiled CGD's recently released Carbon Monitoring for Action (CARMA) online database, which discloses for the first time the carbon dioxide (CO_2) pollution of all power plants and companies in the world.

CARMA shows that the world's biggest CO_2 emitting power plant (Taichung, in Taiwan) and the biggest emitting company (Huaneng Power International, in mainland China) are both in the developing world.

The authors said they calculated separate historical emissions paths for two groups of countries—today's high-income countries in the North and developing countries in the South—by using newly available data for 1850 to 2005.

They projected these trends into the near future using scenarios from the Intergovernmental Panel on Climate Change (IPCC), the international scientific body that won the 2007 Nobel Peace Prize with former U.S. vice president Al Gore, whose film, An Inconvenient Truth, played a significant role in creating awareness about climate change.

According to the CGD projections, by 2040 cumulative emissions from the South alone would drive the atmospheric concentration of CO_2 past the current level of 387 ppm (parts per million)—even without the "contributions" from the North.

By 2060, emissions from the global South could push atmospheric CO_2 past 450 ppm, the threshold that the IPCC links with large, irreversible impacts.

By the end of the century, the atmospheric concentration from the South alone would be nearing 600 ppm, well past the extreme danger zone for catastrophic climate change, according to the study.

Wheeler said these figures are conservative estimates because they do not include other potent greenhouse gases such as methane, nor do they incorporate possible carbon cycle feedback effects—such as soil venting more greenhouse gases as temperatures rise or the oceans absorbing less CO_2 due to increasing acidity or changes in circulation. Many earth scientists warn that these phenomena are already occurring.

In the South, most CO_2 emissions currently come from land use change, primarily deforestation, but emissions from fossil fuels are rising rapidly. In the North, fossil fuels are the primary source of emissions; cumulative emissions from deforestation are actually starting to decline, as some farms in mountainous temperate zones, such as in the Appalachian Mountains in the United States, revert to forest, capturing carbon.

Impact of Rising Temperatures on Agriculture

Other recent studies suggest that the impact of rising temperatures on agriculture will be much more severe for developing countries, which are usually located closer to the equator, than for high-income countries with temperate climates.

William Cline, a joint fellow at CGD and the Peterson Institute for International Economics, warned in a recent book that many developing countries will face steep declines in ag-

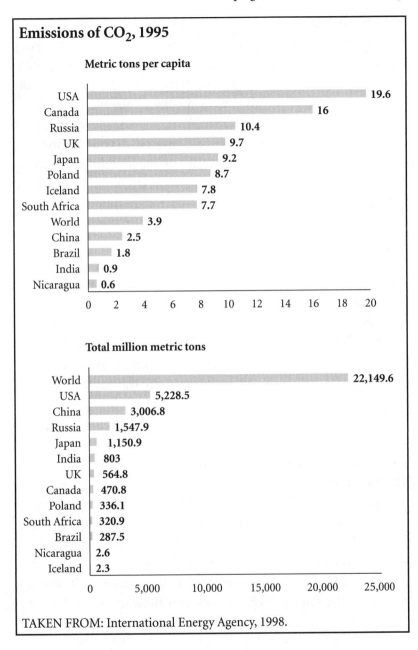

Emissions of CO$_2$, 1995

Metric tons per capita

USA	19.6
Canada	16
Russia	10.4
UK	9.7
Japan	9.2
Poland	8.7
Iceland	7.8
South Africa	7.7
World	3.9
China	2.5
Brazil	1.8
India	0.9
Nicaragua	0.6

0   2   4   6   8   10   12   14   16   18   20

Total million metric tons

World	22,149.6
USA	5,228.5
China	3,006.8
Russia	1,547.9
Japan	1,150.9
India	803
UK	564.8
Canada	470.8
Poland	336.1
South Africa	320.9
Brazil	287.5
Nicaragua	2.6
Iceland	2.3

0   5,000   10,000   15,000   20,000   25,000

TAKEN FROM: International Energy Agency, 1998.

ricultural productivity by 2080 unless global greenhouse emissions are sharply curtailed. Some countries could face agricultural collapse, as higher temperatures interfere with farming.

"Our mission is to provide independent research and practical ideas for global prosperity," said CGD president Nancy Birdsall. "It's crucial that the people and leaders in developing countries, as well as the rich countries, have the best available information about the choices that they confront."

The finding that the South is on its way to creating its own global warming crisis "should not be seen as a cause for complacency in the rich countries, or as somehow absolving us from taking action," she added in a statement. "Instead, we now know that the task is even larger and more daunting than we previously believed."

"To avoid a shared global disaster, we in the rich countries need to cut our own emissions quickly and do much more to help developing countries shift to a low-carbon future, while at the same time meeting the just aspirations of their people for a better life."

Wheeler, a development economist who spent much of his career doing research on developing country environmental issues at the World Bank, confessed in the study to being deeply disturbed by these findings.

"This conclusion is sufficiently startling that the mind gropes for an alternative to such injustice," he said. "Why should the South have fallen into this trap, when the North has somehow managed to avoid it?"

"On reflection, the answer is obvious," Wheeler wrote in the CGD study. "The South's population is over four times greater than the North's, so it has been trapped by the sheer scale of its emissions at a much earlier stage of development. The South finds itself weighed down by a mass of humanity, as well as the energy technologies and fuels of an earlier age."

International Emissions Restrictions May Harm Developing Regions

Hans Martin Seip and Sigbjorn Gronas

The Center for International Climate and Environmental Research (CICERO), based in Oslo, Norway, is an association dedicated to analyzing and promoting international environmental policy. CICERO claims that an increasing number of international organizations seek to reevaluate the climate change issues in economic terms. Many of these organizations, primarily based in the United Kingdom and United States, emphasize market-based and business-based solutions to climate change problems like greenhouse gas emissions. Many are skeptical of the effectiveness of government regulation and international treaties like the Kyoto Protocol. CICERO notes in agreement that the least-developed regions must be permitted to develop, but disagrees that free-market solutions will best balance development with environmental stewardship. Hans Martin Seip is a professor in the chemistry department at the University of Oslo, Norway. Sigbjorn Gronas is a professor of meteorology at the University of Bergen, Norway.

Hans Martin Seip and Sigbjorn Gronas, "Organized Opposition to the Kyoto Protocol," Center for International Climate and Environmental Research, January 2005. Reproduced by permission.

As you read, consider the following questions:

1. What is the title of the International Policy Network's (IPN) climate report?
2. Which two chapters of the report are the most important?
3. What types of nations will be the most vulnerable to climate change?

The UN [United Nations] Framework Convention on Climate Change (UNFCCC) conference in Buenos Aires served as an important reminder that climate policy is a hot issue. Industrial and corporate actors linked to fossil fuels such as coal, oil, and natural gas are worried about their future, and see emissions reduction requirements as a threat. And they are clearly not without influence in the debate. In the United States, they have convinced President George W. Bush to reject the Kyoto Protocol. And in Buenos Aires, the United States went so far as to obstruct attempts to lay the groundwork for additional reductions when the Protocol expires in 2012. The United Kingdom [UK], however, an American ally in many contexts, has elected to pursue greater reductions after 2012.

Business and industry that oppose emissions reductions often work through institutions that organize opposition. Until now, this type of opposition has primarily been seen in the United States. But more recently, the institution International Policy Network (IPN), with offices in the UK, published a climate report. According to its own statutes, the IPN has the noble goal of encouraging respect for people and property, improving human health, and protecting the environment. Despite these fine words, IPN is an institution that unreservedly supports market liberalism. On their home page, they state that IPN believes that market mechanisms and associated organizations are the best instrument for combating poverty and tragedies that affect large numbers of people. IPN brags

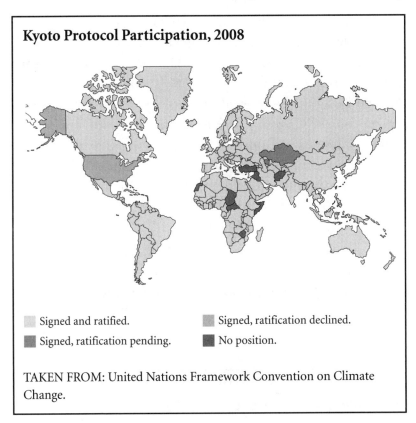

Kyoto Protocol Participation, 2008

Signed and ratified.

Signed, ratification pending.

Signed, ratification declined.

No position.

TAKEN FROM: United Nations Framework Convention on Climate Change.

that they do not accept funding from the government, but only from business and private donors.

IPN's climate report, *The Impacts of Climate Change: An Appraisal of the Future*, has received considerable attention, including in the *Guardian* (Greenhouse Effect 'May Benefit Man', November 28, 2004). The most important chapters are the first two: a debate about the emissions scenarios developed by Intergovernmental Panel on Climate Change (IPCC), and a discussion about the effects of climate change. The report correctly emphasizes the many uncertainties, but generally ignores the uncertain factors that point in the direction of major climate changes. Its faith in cost estimates appears to be great, even though there are numerous examples of costs of environmental measures being lower than originally anticipated.

The first chapter claims that we don't know how sensitive the climate system is to an increase in CO_2 [carbon dioxide]. As recently pointed out in *Nature* there are now good reasons to assume that the climate sensitivity is close to 3°C [Celsius] for a doubling of the concentration of CO_2. It also claims that among the IPCC's many scenarios, the ones with the largest future emissions are unrealistic, suggesting that the IPCC's upper limits for global warming are also unrealistic. Recent research has shown that some of this criticism of the scenarios is of little significance, but we agree that the most pessimistic scenarios are highly unlikely.

Market liberalistic free-trade is proposed as the best instrument for strengthening developing countries and equipping them to face climate changes. Reducing emissions hinders free trade, thus hindering development in poor countries.

Free-Trade Proposed as Tool for Developing Countries

In the second chapter, market liberalistic free-trade is proposed as the best instrument for strengthening developing countries and equipping them to face climate changes. Reducing emissions hinders free trade, thus hindering development in poor countries. A main argument is that the Kyoto Protocol is costly and will only have a marginal effect on global warming. This is true to a certain extent, even though the agreement will reduce the probability for the most pessimistic emissions scenarios. More important is that the agreement hopefully represents the beginning of a process that will lead to more ambitious reductions. To put a twist on [Winston] Churchill's famous words: The Kyoto Protocol is not the end. It is not even the beginning of the end. But it is perhaps the end of the beginning.

It is expected that poor countries will be the most vulnerable to climate changes because poverty makes it difficult to adapt to changes. Thus, the report claims that it must be better to spend money on fighting poverty and disease directly than to use money to reduce greenhouse gas emissions. This is similar to the way [Bjorn] Lomborg's project "the Copenhagen Consensus" pits worthy causes up against one another. No one disagrees that it is important to fight malaria, but such efforts need not stand in the way of reducing emissions. It is claimed that "alternative approaches all of which rely on improving adaptation and reducing vulnerability, are superior to the single-minded pursuit of reductions of climate change." Who wants this kind of single-mindedness?

The report does not reject the notion of global warming, but little weight is given to arguments for limiting emissions— for example, that the impacts of greenhouse gases last for hundreds of years, and that in the long run we cannot disregard surprises such as rapid, dramatic climate changes.

Of course we agree that poverty must be combated, and that higher standards of living make it easier to protect against climate changes. But we also have to reduce emissions. The report has no other prescription for how poverty can be fought than "business as usual." Thus the report is merely a defense for unreserved market liberalism and free emissions of greenhouse gases.

China's Rapid Development Raises Global Levels of Greenhouse Gas Emissions

The Economist

The following viewpoint from The Economist *evaluates the environmental perils created by growth and development. The article focuses on the connections among China's rapid economic development, rising fuel and energy consumption, and increasing greenhouse gas emissions. Air pollution accompanies the building boom in the capital city of Beijing; in the provinces, air quality is compromised by new coal-burning power plants. Rivers that supply water to the nation's large population centers are running dry.* The Economist, *based in London, England, is a magazine focusing on international economic and policy issues.*

As you read, consider the following questions:

1. In 2003, China's electricity consumption surged so unexpectedly that China began suffering from what?

2. How many square kilometers of ocean off China's shores have been contaminated by polluted rivers?

3. On average, cars in China are how much more efficient than cars in America?

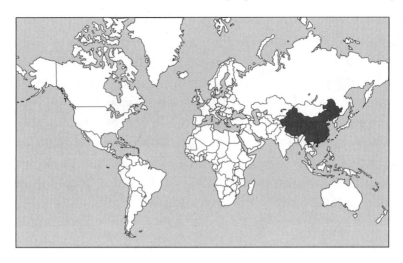

China will not continue to grow at the same pace as it has done recently, or suck in as many raw materials, if its leaders get their way. The 11th Five-Year Plan, which lays out their main economic goals for the period from 2006 to 2010, calls for growth to slow to 7.5% a year from its current double-digit pace and for consumption of energy—a good proxy for resources in general—to decelerate even more.

The government has several motives for stepping on the brakes. One is simply to allow its bureaucrats time to plan for and direct growth. Its chief aim is to redress the growing inequality between the prosperous coastal provinces and the poorer interior ones, and between cities and the countryside. But slower, more carefully orchestrated growth might also avoid wasteful and disruptive bottlenecks.

In 2003, for example, electricity consumption surged so unexpectedly that China began suffering from repeated brownouts as the grid ran short of power. That prompted millions to buy diesel generators, which in turn led to a 10% jump in oil imports in 2004. Since then, electricity companies have been building power stations with gay abandon. In 2005 and 2006, they added more generating capacity than France has in total. That has boosted demand for coal, since most of the new plants are coal-fired. But most of China's coal comes from the country's interior and must be transported to coastal power stations by train. That is using up a lot of diesel (on which the trains run) and clogging up the rail network. So power stations have begun shipping in coal from overseas, turning China into a net importer in the first half of 2007, and prompting the huge queues of freighters outside coal ports such as Newcastle, Australia. These lurches in demand for different resources have added to the jitters in commodity markets and helped to amplify price rises.

Processing iron ore, timber or oil requires electricity, and 80% of China's electricity comes from coal. But the sulphur that spews from the smokestacks of coal-fired power stations causes acid rain and the soot generates smog.

The government is also worried about security of supplies. Senior figures still daydream about self-sufficiency, looking back to Maoist doctrine and to the terrible man-made famine of the late 1950s. They fret, too, that foreigners might attempt to blockade the country in the event of a war over Taiwan. In particular, the government is anxious about its oil imports from the Middle East and Africa, all of which pass through the narrow Singapore Strait. So it has been pushing for alternative routes, such as a pipeline from Kazakhstan, which opened in 2006, and another one from Russia, which has been under discussion for the past decade. The government has also created, and started filling, a strategic reserve, which should eventually hold 30 days' worth of imports, says the IEA [International Energy Agency].

The environmental fallout from China's burgeoning demand for natural resources is another source of concern. Processing iron ore, timber or oil requires electricity, and 80% of China's electricity comes from coal. But the sulphur that spews from the smokestacks of coal-fired power stations causes acid rain and the soot generates smog. In many Chinese cities, a thick shroud of pollution literally blots out the sun much of the time. Acid rain, meanwhile, reduces agricultural yields and eats away at buildings and infrastructure. The OECD cites a finding that air pollution alone reduces the country's output by between 3% and 7% a year, mainly because of respiratory ailments that keep workers at home.

A Dry Subject

China's water supply, too, is in a parlous state, thanks to ever-increasing industrial and agricultural use. The amount of water available per head of population is only a quarter of the global average. In the arid north and west of the country that figure falls to a tenth. Two in three cities already suffer from shortages. Groundwater is being pumped out much faster than it is being replenished.

Not even Beijing treats all its sewage; other cities treat none at all. Famous beauty spots, such as Taihu Lake near Shanghai, are often afflicted by hideous algal blooms, while effluent from polluted rivers has contaminated 160,000 square kilometres of ocean off China's shores, officials say. Over half the water in the seven biggest river basins is unfit for consumption, according to a recent report from the World Bank. The resulting health problems reduce rural output by 2%, it found, and the costs to industry and agriculture of dirty and scarce water sap GDP [gross domestic product] by another percentage point.

The Himalayan glaciers that feed China's biggest rivers ... are melting.

All told, the World Bank put the price tag for China's air and water pollution at $100 billion a year, or about 5.8% of GDP. It is said that the same report originally put the number of deaths caused by the two scourges at 750,000 a year—until the Chinese government complained and asked for the figure to be removed. Pan Yue, a deputy minister at the State Environmental Protection Administration (SEPA), China's paramount environmental regulator, estimates the annual cost of environmental damage at 8–13% of GDP—much the same as the overall economic growth rate. If it continues like this, he expects levels of pollution to double over the next 15 years.

Then there is global warming, which is already exacerbating China's environmental problems. The latest report from the Intergovernmental Panel on Climate Change [IPCC] notes that temperatures in China are rising and extreme weather, including cyclones, droughts and floods, is on the increase. Worse, the Himalayan glaciers that feed China's biggest rivers (and account for a large portion of flows during dry spells) are melting. "If the present rate continues," the report says, "the likelihood of them disappearing by the year 2035 and perhaps sooner is very high."

Among other things, this will make life even more difficult for China's farmers. Northern China, which lost some 36,000 square kilometres to desertification between 1990 and 2000, will become even more arid. Its water supply, the IPCC predicts, will fall 30% below requirements. Moreover, rice yields will drop by 10% for every degree the temperature increases. Rising sea levels and the associated intrusion of salt water are likely to reduce the amount of arable land even further.

As it is, in villages like Beihuadan, in Hebei province, just a few hours' drive from Beijing, the water table is already falling rapidly. A shuffling farmer in a flat cap and worn woolen sweater pumps furiously at the well in the courtyard of his house to show that it has run dry. It is only 19 metres deep, he explains, but there is no water these days for at least 70 metres, and often not for 100 metres or more. A few houses away a group of old men interrupt a game of cards to point out another dry well. For five years, they say, there has been no water in the Beijuma River, which runs past the edge of the village, and the authorities do not provide adequate alternative supplies through the local irrigation network.

The government is planning to invest billions in a system of canals, pipelines and aqueducts to divert water from the soggy south to the parched north. But the scheme is only a temporary fix, and is just the sort of grandiose engineering project that tends to cause environmental problems of its own. Many NGOs [nongovernmental organizations] and hydrologists are adamantly opposed.

As it is, the environment is the second most frequent subject of public protests after disputes over land, according to Mr Pan [Yue]. In 2005, the authorities recorded 50,000 such protests, he says, and that was a 30% increase on the year before. Last year, 10,000 people turned out to demonstrate against a planned chemical plant in the city of Xiamen. Earlier this year, hundreds of Shanghainese protested against a proposed extension to the city's maglev train, worried about health risks. Such protests are particularly unnerving for the authorities because they involve educated, articulate and well-organised urbanites, not the country folk who normally suffer most from abuse by officials.

The best response to all these worries is to encourage more sparing use of resources, and that is what the government is trying to do. The current five-year plan, which contains few other numerical targets, envisages a 10% reduction in concentrations of the worst air pollutants and a 20% increase in energy efficiency over the period. The central government has assigned specific energy-efficiency goals to each of China's 1,000 biggest enterprises and encouraged lower levels of government to do the equivalent.

The government has set relatively stringent fuel-economy standards for cars, as well as minimum energy-efficiency requirements for all manner of appliances. On average, cars in China are about 50% more efficient than in America. Subsidies on energy consumption have also been falling steadily.

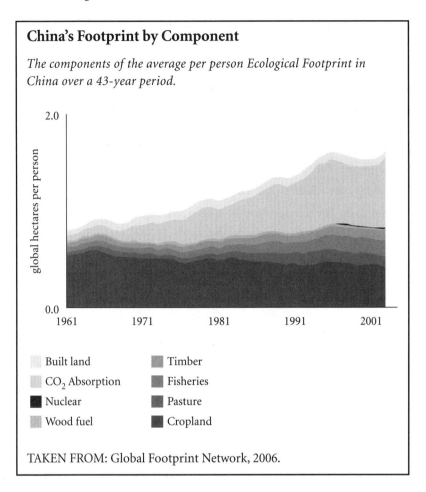

China's Footprint by Component

The components of the average per person Ecological Footprint in China over a 43-year period.

Built land
CO_2 Absorption
Nuclear
Wood fuel

Timber
Fisheries
Pasture
Cropland

TAKEN FROM: Global Footprint Network, 2006.

The IEA calculates that their total value in 2006 was roughly $11 billion, less than half the amount for 2005. That is all the more remarkable given that international oil, coal, and natural gas prices were rising rapidly at the time. Petrol prices, for example, have been going up even faster for Chinese drivers than they have for Americans or Europeans, although they remain low in absolute terms.

To discourage energy- and import-intensive metals-processing, the government raised export duties on iron, steel and related alloys to 25% in December [2007]. It also abolished all duty on imports of copper, in the hope that higher imports of finished metal might displace some domestic smelting. And on two previous occasions it has reduced the level of tax rebates that exporters of energy-intensive goods can claim, in some cases down to zero.

There is also a move to diversify away from coal. In big cities (especially Beijing, in preparation for the [2008 Summer] Olympics), coal-fired heating and power plants are having to be modified to run on natural gas. In the Beijing suburb of Fengtai, where the switch has already taken place, residents recall how the constant dusting of soot from the power plant used to stop them from drying clothes outdoors or even opening their windows. Now they can hang out their washing without fear, and sometimes even sit outside.

Nuclear Options

The government is planning to increase the country's nuclear generation capacity almost fivefold by 2020. It has ordered new reactors from two of the world's nuclear giants, Areva and Westinghouse, and is also building some of its own design. Power from wind turbines is meant to double by 2010 and grow by a factor of 12% by 2020. Hydropower is supposed almost to triple by the same date. Overall, renewable sources should account for 15% of energy consumption by 2020.

At the same time SEPA is trying to clean up China's coal-fired plants. All new ones are required to install filters in their smokestacks to remove sulphur dioxide, the main cause of acid rain. The biggest existing plants are supposed to retrofit such equipment. Roughly half of China's coal-fired generating capacity is now said to have installed this kind of technology. Between 2000 and 2005, SEPA tripled the fines on polluters. The government has also hired Veolia, a French conglomerate, to build and run model waste-water treatment plants in several big cities.

An Open-and-Shut Case

As the big power plants, factories and coal mines raise their environmental standards, the small ones are meant to shut down altogether. Cyrille Ragoucy, the local head of Lafarge, a cement giant, says that the authorities have encouraged the firm to expand rapidly in the south-west of the country in order to replace the existing stock of old-fashioned, energy-intensive and polluting cement kilns. At the same time, local governments have been ordered to close coal-fired power plants with a capacity of less than 25 MW [megawatts] and to bar the construction of any new plants of less than 300 MW. The larger scale, along with more modern technology, should improve efficiency dramatically. All told, the government plans to close 50,000 MW-worth of small plants by 2010.

The biggest push concerns small coal mines, in which thousands of workers perish every year. They also tend to produce poor-quality coal, which generates relatively high levels of pollution when burned. In addition, many of the mines contaminate local water supplies and produce unhealthy, smog-inducing dust in great quantities. So the central government has instructed local officials to shut down any small, dirty and unsafe mines. According to Xinhua, China's state-run news agency, 11,155 such facilities have been closed since the campaign started in 2005. The government wants to eliminate another 4,000 by the end of this year [2008].

But a visit to the province of Shanxi, in the heart of China's coal belt, reveals why such plans should be taken with a pinch of salt. The Jinhuagong mine, a spokesman explains, is something of a model. It produces 4 m tonnes of high-quality coal a year, using the latest British and German machinery. There have been no fatal accidents for two years. The mine's managers are so proud of it that they have opened it up to tourists. Visitors can dress up in jumpsuits and hard hats and descend in a creaking elevator to the coalface 300 metres below the surface. There, a bone-jarring miniature train hauls them a few kilometres deeper into the mine, where they can look at an exhibition on the gradual improvements in safety standards over the years. All the mines in the area that did not comply with safety regulations, the spokesman explains, have been closed.

Yet a taxi driver hailed outside Jinhuagong's gates says he knows of plenty of mines that remain open in defiance of the central government's orders. Waving at Shanxi's bleak landscape of barren, eroded hillsides and jagged valleys, he says: "There's coal everywhere. Wherever there's a road, there's a coalmine." Sure enough, a half-hour drive through the hills reveals several tiny operations where jerry-rigged conveyor belts carry coal to waiting lorries and workers scatter at the sight of an inquisitive foreigner.

The incentive to continue mining is overwhelming, locals explain. The same shortage of coal that is driving up imports has also pushed up the price. In January [2008], power companies had to shut several coal-fired plants because they did not have enough fuel to go round. The government has withdrawn all export credits on coal and imposed taxes instead, but supply continues to fall short of demand. Moreover, the officials who are responsible for closing mines are often shareholders in them too. And even if they have no financial interest in them, they still view economic growth and job creation as the chief gauge of their success.

Even those plants that have the equipment to remove sulphur dioxide from their flue gas often do not bother . . . because the process uses power and so reduces profits.

The Intentions Are Good

SEPA did come up with an alternative yardstick, dubbed "green GDP" and intended as a joint measure of both environmental and economic stewardship. But sceptical [skeptical] officials rebelled, so the central government quietly shelved the scheme. Regulators concede that poor enforcement is undermining most of their attempts to improve the state of the environment. SEPA has less than a tenth of the staff of its American equivalent to police a country with over four times the population. To enforce its rulings, it relies on local bureaucrats over whom it has no authority. "Overall, environmental efforts have lacked effectiveness and efficiency, largely as a result of an implementation gap," as the OECD's report puts it.

That is why Jim Brock, a consultant to domestic and foreign energy firms in China, thinks it is unlikely that many small power plants are in fact being closed down. Even those plants that have the equipment to remove sulphur dioxide from their flue gas often do not bother, officials concede, because the process uses power and so reduces profits. At any rate, emissions are not yet falling fast enough to meet the government's targets.

What is more, the proliferation of coal-fired plants is swamping the growth in renewable power. Some 90% of the power plants built in 2006 run on coal, the IEA notes, against 70% of those built in 2000. And heavy industry such as steel-making continues to grow, says Rui Susheng, the director of the China Coal Society, despite the government's attempts to curb it.

All this means that the government is falling short of its energy-efficiency targets. In 2006, China's energy intensity (the ratio of energy consumption to economic output) fell by 1.2%, well-short of the government's goal of 4% a year until 2010. That was an improvement on the previous few years, when it actually rose. Yet the impression remains that the government is fighting a losing battle.

Periodical Bibliography

The following articles have been selected to supplement the diverse views presented in this chapter.

Sabihuddin Ahmed	"We Are The Ones Who Will Pay for the Damage," *The Independent*, February 19, 2007.
Bob Butler	"Climate Change Reduces Fish Stocks in Senegal," *Oakland Tribune*, January 2, 2008.
Lewis Cleverdon	"Environmental Genocide," *New Internationalist*, May 1, 2006.
Steven Connor	"No One Is Immune from the Effects of Climate Change," *The Independent*, November 30, 2005.
Neil Ford	"Seeking Water Solutions for Africa," *African Business*, January 1, 2008.
Andrew Grice	"Global Warming 'Will Cancel Out Western Aid and Devastate Africa,'" *The Independent*, July 13, 2006.
Michael McCarthy	"Global Warming Identified as Greatest Threat to World's Poor," *The Independent*, October 21, 2004.
Tom Okello	"Feeling the Heat," *The New African*, July 1, 2005.
Gene J. Pfeffer	"We Must Adapt To, Not Fight Climate Change," *The Gazette* (Colorado Springs), November 14, 2007.
Lauren Sacks	"Climate Change and Food Security," April 6, 2007. www.climate.org.
Randolph E. Schmid	"'Great Dying' Linked to Global Warming," *Deseret News* (Salt Lake City), January 21, 2005.
The World Bank	"Developing Countries Brace for Climate Change Impact," 2007. www.worldbank.org.

Combating Global Climate Change

Worldwide Tree Planting Project Aims to Offset Some Emissions

United Nations Environment Programme

The United Nations Environment Programme (UNEP) has coordinated the "Plant for the Planet: Billion Tree Campaign." This campaign encourages all sectors of society to help battle climate change by planting trees, whether it be in one of four key areas identified by UNEP or in the backyard. According to UNEP, forests are continually being destroyed for agricultural purposes, and only a small fraction remains undisturbed by human interference. The United Nations' "Plant for the Planet" program hopes to combat deforestation by meeting its objective of planting at least 1 billion trees worldwide each year.

The mission of UNEP is to encourage caring for the environment by inspiring, informing, and enabling people to improve their quality of life without compromising that of future generations.

As you read, consider the following questions:

1. What are the four key areas the campaign encourages for tree planting?
2. How much of the world is forested areas?
3. What is the definition of a "primary forest?"

The Plant for the Planet: Billion Tree Campaign, coordinated by the United Nations Environment Programme (UNEP), will encourage all sectors of society—from the concerned citizen to the philanthropic corporation—to take small but practical steps to combat what is probably the key challenge of the 21st century.

The campaign, backed by Nobel Peace Prize laureate and Green Belt Movement activist Professor Wangari Maathai; His Serene Highness Albert II, Sovereign Prince of Monaco; and the World Agroforestry Centre-ICRAF, was unveiled at the annual climate change convention conference taking place in Nairobi.

Achim Steiner, United Nations Under-Secretary-General and Executive Director of UNEP, said: "Intergovernmental talks on addressing climate change can often be difficult, protracted and sometimes frustrating, especially for those looking on but we cannot and must not lose heart".

"Meanwhile, action does not need to be confined to the corridors of the negotiation halls. The campaign, which aims to plant a minimum of one billion trees in 2007, offers a direct and straightforward path down which all sectors of society can step to contribute to meeting the climate change challenge," he added.

"In re-creating lost forests and developing new ones, we can also address other concerns including loss of biodiversity, improving water availability, stemming desertification and reducing erosion," said Mr Steiner.

If everyone in the United Kingdom switched off rather than left TV sets and other appliances on standby, it would save enough electricity to power close to three million homes for a year.

Professor Maathai said: "When we are planting trees sometimes people will say to me, 'I don't want to plant this tree, because it will not grow fast enough'. I have to keep reminding them that the trees they are cutting today were not planted by them, but by those who came before. So they must plant the trees that will benefit communities in the future."

Mr Steiner added: "The Billion Tree Campaign is but an acorn, but it can also be practically and symbolically a significant expression of our common determination to make a difference in developing and developed countries alike."

"We have but a short time to avert serious climate change. We need action. We need to plant trees alongside other concrete community-minded actions and in doing so, send a signal to the corridors of political power across the globe that the watching and waiting is over—that countering climate change can take root via one billion small but significant acts in our gardens, parks, countryside and rural areas," said Mr Steiner.

Other actions include people driving less, switching off lights in empty rooms and turning off electrical appliances rather than leaving them on standby. If everyone in the United Kingdom switched off rather than left TV sets and other appliances on standby, it would save enough electricity to power close to three million homes for a year, according to some estimates.

Where the "Plant a Billion Trees" Idea Originated

The idea for Plant for the Planet: Billion Tree Campaign was inspired by Professor Maathai who, along with the Prince, is co-patron of the new initiative.

When a corporate group in the United States told Professor Maathai it was planning to plant a million trees, her response was: "That's great, but what we really need is to plant a billion trees."

His Serene Highness Albert II, said: "I am particularly honoured to be associated with the founder, Professor Wangari

Maathai, whose involvement in the process of reforestation has been, and continues to be, inspirational. To plant a tree for future generations is a simple gesture, yet a strong symbol of sustainable development."

Under the Plant for the Planet: Billion Tree Campaign, people and entities from around the world are encouraged to enter pledges on a Web site www.unep.org/billiontree campaign.

The campaign is open to all—individuals, children and youth groups, schools, community groups, non-governmental organizations, farmers, private sector organizations, local authorities, and national governments. Each pledge can be anything from a single tree to 10 million trees.

The Plant for the Planet: Billion Tree Campaign encourages the planting of indigenous trees and trees that are appropriate to the local environment, with mixtures of species preferred over other options.

The campaign identifies four key areas for planting: degraded natural forests and wilderness areas; farms and rural landscapes; sustainably managed plantations; and urban environments, but it can also begin with a single tree in a back garden.

Advice on tree planting will be made available via the Web site, as well as information about reforestation and other tree-related issues, including links to appropriate partner organizations best equipped to give locally tailored advice, such as the World Agroforestry Centre-ICRAF.

Dennis Garrity, ICRAF Director General, said: "The Plant for the Planet: Billion Tree Campaign is a superb initiative by UNEP to link people, trees and the environment. Planting trees is great, although using appropriate scientific knowledge to plant the right tree in the right place is even greater. The 500 million smallholder farmers in the tropics stand to benefit tremendously from the greater recognition, appreciation and

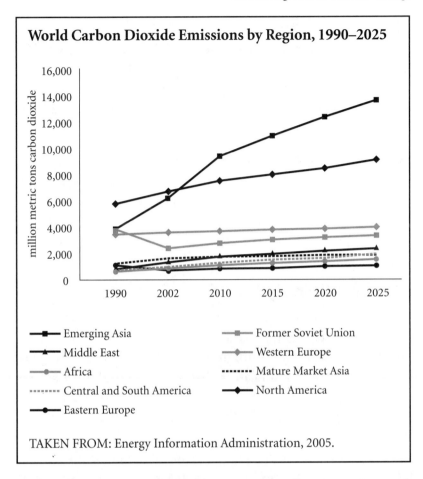

World Carbon Dioxide Emissions by Region, 1990–2025

Legend:
- ■ Emerging Asia
- ▲ Middle East
- ● Africa
- ┈ Central and South America
- ● Eastern Europe
- ■ Former Soviet Union
- ◆ Western Europe
- ┈ Mature Market Asia
- ◆ North America

TAKEN FROM: Energy Information Administration, 2005.

promotion of the right trees in the right places, so that such trees may transform both lives and landscapes."

The responsibility for tree planting will lie with the person or organization making the pledge via the campaign Web site. All contributing participants to the Billion Tree Campaign will receive a certificate of involvement.

They will be encouraged to follow up via the Web site so UNEP can verify that the trees have survived, in partnership with recognized certification mechanisms. The Web site will record the ongoing tally of pledges, and also publish photos and accounts from registered campaign members of what they have achieved. . . .

How Much of the World Is Forested?

Forests cover 30 per cent of the planet's total land area. The total forested area in 2005 was just under 4 billion hectares, at least one third less than before the dawn of agriculture, some 10,000 years ago. (100 hectares is the same as 1 square kilometre).

Where Are Most Forests Found?

Forests are unevenly distributed. The ten most forest-rich countries, which account for two-thirds of the total forested area, are the Russian Federation, Brazil, Canada, the United States, China, Australia, Democratic Republic of Congo, Indonesia, Peru and India.

What Is a Primary Forest?

On a global average, more than one-third of all forests are primary forests, defined as forests where there are no clearly visible indications of human activity and where ecological processes are not significantly disturbed. Six million hectares of primary forest are lost every year due to deforestation and modification through selective logging and other human interventions.

Only 20 per cent of the world's forests remain in large, intact areas. These forests consist of tropical rain forests, mangrove, coastal and swamp forests. Monsoon and deciduous forests flourish in the drier and more mountainous regions. Primary forests shelter diverse animal and plant species, and culturally diverse indigenous people, with deep connections to their habitat.

What Are the Protective Functions of Forests?

Trees quite literally form the foundations of many natural systems. They help to conserve soil and water, control avalanches, prevent desertification, protect coastal areas and stabilize sand dunes.

Forests are the most important repositories of terrestrial biological biodiversity, housing up to 90 per cent of known terrestrial species.

Trees and shrubs play a vital role in the daily life of rural communities. They provide sources of timber, fuel wood, food, fodder, essential oils, gums, resins and latex, medicines and shade. Forest animals have a vital role in forest ecology such as pollination, seed dispersal and germination.

What Are the Links Between Forests and Climate Change?

Trees absorb carbon dioxide and are vital carbon sinks. It is estimated that the world's forests store 283 gigatonnes of carbon in their biomass alone, and that carbon stored in forest biomass, deadwood, litter and soil together is roughly 50 per cent more than the carbon in the atmosphere.

Carbon in forest biomass decreased in Africa, Asia and South America in the period 1990–2005. For the world as a whole, carbon stocks in forest biomass decreased annually by 1.1 gigatonne of carbon (equivalent to 4 billion 25 kg [kilogram] sacks of charcoal).

The loss of natural forests around the world contributes more to global emissions each year than the transport sector. Curbing deforestation is a highly cost-effective way to reduce emissions.

Other solutions include increased energy efficiency, reduced energy demand, better transport and the use of green energy.

What Is the Deforestation Rate on Earth?

World population currently stands at 6.5 billion people. It is projected to grow to 9 billion by 2042. The expansion of agricultural and industrial needs, population growth, poverty, landlessness and consumer demand are the major driving forces behind deforestation. Most deforestation is due to conversion of forests to agricultural land. Global removals of wood for timber and fuel amounted to 3.1 billion cubic metres in 2005.

Worldwide, deforestation continues at an alarming rate, about 13 million hectares per year, an area the size of Greece or Nicaragua. Africa and South America have the largest net loss of forests. In Africa, it is estimated that nearly half of forest loss was due to removal of wood fuel. Forests in Europe are expanding. Asia, which had a net loss in the 1990s, reported a net gain of forests in the past five years, primarily due to large-scale forestation in China.

Forest planting and the natural expansion of forests help to reduce the net loss of forests. The net change in forested area in the period 2000–2005 is estimated at 7.3 million hectares a year (an area about the size of Sierra Leone or Panama), down from 8.9 million hectares a year in the period 1990–2000.

Where Should Trees Be Planted As a Priority?

Favourable growing conditions give nations in the southern hemisphere an advantage over most industrial countries in the economics of wood production. Plantations in the south can produce 10–20 cubic metres of wood per hectare per year, considerably more than plantations in most northern temperate regions and 10–20 times the typical productivity of natural forests worldwide.

The Plant for the Planet: Billion Tree Campaign encourages the planting of trees in four key areas, namely: (i) degraded natural forests and wilderness areas; (ii) farms and rural landscapes; (iii) sustainably managed plantations; and (iv) urban environments. Trees have to be well adapted to local conditions, and mixtures of species are preferred over monocultures. Many trees have communal benefits, especially for the poor, and ownership, access and use rights are as important as the number of trees.

Who Owns Forests and Trees?

Forest and tree ownership and tenure are changing. Eighty per cent of the world's forests are publicly owned, but private ownership is on the rise, especially in North and Central America and in Oceania.

About 11 per cent of the world's forests are designated for the conservation of biological diversity.

These areas are mainly, but not exclusively, in protected areas.

Who Cares for Forests and Trees?

Around 10 million people are employed in conventional forest management and conservation. Formal employment in forestry declined by about 10 per cent from 1990 to 2000. More than 1 billion forest adjacent people are informal custodians of forests. They rely on forest products and services for a significant part of their livelihoods. Approximately 500 million small-scale farmers in the tropics retain and manage trees on their farms for livelihood goals.

Without trees, human life would be unsustainable.

Trees and Humanity

Forests provide not only environmental protection, but also significant income and livelihood options globally for more than one billion forest-dependent people.

Trees provide a wide range of products (timber, fruit, medicine, beverages, fodder) and services (carbon sequestration, shade, beautification, erosion control, soil fertility). Without trees, human life would be unsustainable.

Forests also play an important cultural, spiritual and recreational role in many societies. In some cases, they are integral to the very definition and survival of indigenous and traditional cultures.

Forests and trees are symbolically important in most of the world's major religions. Trees symbolize historical continuity, they link earth and heavens and, to many traditions, are home to both good and bad spirits and the souls of ancestors.

Forests also play an important role in offering recreational opportunities and spiritual solace in modern societies. They are universally powerful symbols, a physical expression of life, growth and vigour to urban, rural and forest dwellers alike.

Medicinal products from trees help to cure diseases and increase fertility. Aspirin originally came from the bark of a willow tree. Quinine, the cure for malaria, comes from the bark of Cinchona trees.

Trees preside over community discussions and marriages. They are planted at the birth of a child and at burial sites.

Information Technology Companies Can Take Action Against Climate Change

Michael Dell

Michael Dell reports that world energy consumption is on the rise and that corporations and offices need to do something to curtail carbon emissions. Dell suggests that office equipment alone will account for a notable percentage of total energy consumption in Great Britain by 2020. Within larger companies it will be up to committed individuals to begin reducing carbon emissions, and start lessening their corporations' carbon footprints. Michael Dell is the founder and CEO of Dell, one of the world's most profitable computer companies.

As you read, consider the following questions:

1. How many trees does Dell project it saves by using recycled paper?
2. According to a United Kingdom study, office equipment is projected to account for how much total energy use by 2020?
3. What does Dell's "Plant a Tree for Me" program entail?

The global information technology industry has been a catalyst for innovation and opportunity since the days of the first microcomputer. Information technology transformed global commerce by making it much easier to manage information, communicate, research, play and shop.

The ever-accelerating pace of innovation also created the need for manufacturers to look at—and deal with—the entire lifecycle of the technology they created.

Today's customer—armed with a wealth of knowledge and research on what is and is not beneficial for the world's natural resources—fully expects us to do a better job forecasting and managing our companies' impact.

According to the most recent estimates from the Energy Information Administration, a branch of the US [United States] government, world energy consumption is projected to rise 71 per cent from 2003 to 2030. At the same time, carbon dioxide emissions are expected to grow at an average rate of 2.1 per cent a year.

Nowhere is this more evident than in international efforts to reduce energy demand and greenhouse gas emissions. The days when businesses could send a product into the marketplace without first considering how it might affect the environment are over.

And for good reason. According to the most recent estimates from the Energy Information Administration, a branch of the US [United States] government, world energy consumption is projected to rise 71 per cent from 2003 to 2030. At the same time, carbon dioxide emissions are expected to grow at an average rate of 2.1 per cent a year.

My company was founded with the vision that customers could be best served through direct relationships. Twenty-three years later, the direct relationship—now a cornerstone of many companies—can be one of our most valuable tools in collective efforts to reduce energy consumption and protect the environment.

Our success will depend on our ability to empower customers to join us in making a difference. From energy-efficiency to offsetting carbon emissions to reuse and recycling, we must work together to generate immediate and long-term results. Taking steps now to remove any remaining barriers—such as expanding no-charge recycling to consumers all over the world, as Dell has done—will help us get these results. When a programme is simple and the customer is part of the solution, good things happen.

Three Key Areas of Focus

As we continue to improve the efficiencies of IT [information technology] products, reduce the harmful materials used in them, and co-operate to dispose of old products properly through recycling programmes, we should focus on three key areas.

First, we can make protecting the environment easier. Initiatives that are time-consuming, hidden, and expensive only discourage participation. Creating easy and low-cost opportunities for businesses—where businesses take ownership of what they make and sell—will strengthen commitment to protecting the environment.

Dell, for example, offers global recycling and product recovery programmes for customers, with participation requiring little effort on their part. As a result, we are ahead of our goal of recovering 275m pounds of used computer equipment from customers worldwide by 2009.

In addition, we estimate that use of recycled paper in our catalogues avoids the consumption of nearly 35,000 tons of virgin fibre and saves 250,000 trees.

Second, we should tap every creative approach to lessen the environmental impact throughout a product's lifecycle. This starts with design and ends when the product is no longer wanted.

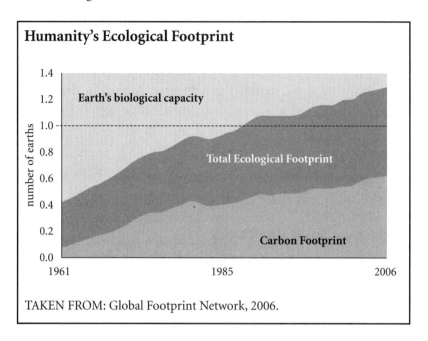

Humanity's Ecological Footprint

Earth's biological capacity

Total Ecological Footprint

Carbon Footprint

number of earths

1.4
1.2
1.0
0.8
0.6
0.4
0.2
0.0

1961   1985   2006

TAKEN FROM: Global Footprint Network, 2006.

Consumers of the digital age have the luxury of picking and choosing like never before. This freedom of choice means that consumers look beyond basic features of products or services to other important factors, such as buying from companies with energy-efficient products and utilising new IT capabilities to achieve greater efficiency and output from fewer products.

A recent study funded by the UK [United Kingdom] government found that office equipment is projected to account for 30 per cent of total energy use in the country by 2020, with PC monitors and system units accounting for about 65 per cent of that. We should always help our customers take advantage of the latest in energy-saving technology, including easy-to-use online digital calculators that help them estimate their power needs.

In many companies, the worst offenders in consuming a large amount of electricity are legacy systems.

Upgrading hardware often makes sense, as newer products are generally more energy-efficient as well as easier to maintain and more productive. Dell's latest servers, for example, consume up to 25 per cent less energy than previous generations, saving hundreds of dollars a year on each system in energy costs. And our new desktop computers use up to 70 per cent less power than previous models.

In addition, there are benefits to investing in techniques such as server consolidation and virtualisation (the hosting of multiple independent operating systems on a single server). These are more energy-efficient and make better use of existing hardware.

Virtualisation allows the data centre to run as efficiently as possible by ensuring that each asset is better utilised, thereby doing more with less power. Fewer servers are needed, making distinct savings in power, space, cooling and administration.

Third, we will only benefit by embracing governments as partners. Legislatures need only look at the success of the marketplace in developing fresh ideas to promote environmental stewardship.

Legislative or regulatory mandates that threaten to undermine the progress made to date should simply be dropped. Meanwhile, businesses and consumers are in a unique position to find common solutions on the environment and global climate change.

Every Consumer Can Participate

One of many examples of unregulated leadership is Dell's "Plant a Tree for Me Program" announced this year and being launched soon in the UK and continental Europe. It reduces the impact of carbon dioxide emissions from computers by offering customers the opportunity to offset the emissions associated with the generation of electricity used to power their machines by making a contribution to buying a tree when they buy their PC [personal computer].

Within the company, we are also finding ways to enhance operational efficiencies, while reducing our carbon footprint through the use of renewable energy.

American anthropologist Margaret Mead once said: "Never doubt that a small group of thoughtful, committed citizens can change the world. Indeed, it's the only thing that ever has."

The same entrepreneurial spirit and innovation that led to automobiles and the personal computer can bring new environmental-friendly ventures. Every consumer can participate. Every company can make a difference. Our work is only just starting.

Australia's Government Bans Traditional Light Bulbs

Wendy Frew and Linton Besser

The Australian government is committed to phasing out incandescent light bulbs and replacing them with compact fluorescent bulbs, which last much longer than the outdated bulbs currently being used. The federal government estimates that replacing old bulbs with compact fluorescent bulbs can drastically reduce greenhouse gas emissions. According to the authors, incandescent bulbs were not developed to curtail greenhouse gas emissions, and with this outdated technology, as much as 95 percent of the energy from incandescent bulbs is wasted.

Wendy Frew and Linton Besser write for the Sydney Morning Herald, *one of Australia's oldest daily newspapers, founded in 1841 by John Fairfax.*

As you read, consider the following questions:

1. Typically, compact fluorescent light bulbs last how many times longer than their predecessors?
2. In Australia, lighting represents what percentage of greenhouse gas emissions from households?
3. When were incandescent light bulbs first developed?

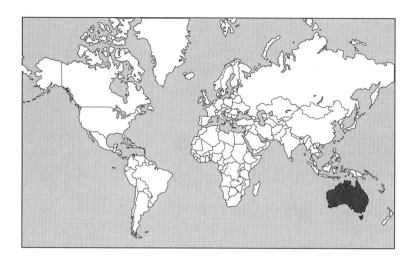

The inefficient standard light bulb could be phased out within three years to save up to 800,000 tonnes of greenhouse gas emissions.

The federal Environment Minister, Malcolm Turnbull, is expected today to announce a commitment to phase out incandescent light bulbs by 2009–10, a world first by a national government.

It hopes to convince state and territory governments to introduce energy performance standards that would lead to the replacement of standard light bulbs with more efficient but more expensive alternatives such as compact fluorescent lights. It will also negotiate with manufacturers to phase out the bulbs.

Though the days of supermarket shelves full of 40-cent light bulbs may be numbered, the lighting industry predicts the price shock will not last long. In many cases, compact fluorescent lamps [light bulbs] sell for about $10 each, but typically last six times as long as their predecessors.

Colin Goldman, the head of Nelson Industries, a lighting importer, supported the move.

"These days you can buy a six-pack at the $10 mark," he said. "The prices are coming down, and as soon as you get volume with greater numbers on the market they come down further."

The Government is under pressure to improve its green credentials. Climate change will be a big issue in the federal election.

Energy Australia says by using just one 15-watt compact fluorescent bulb instead of a 75-watt standard bulb, consumers could save about $10 a year.

The Switch to Compact Fluorescent Bulbs

Australia was not the first with the idea. Last month legislators in California proposed a "How Many Legislators Does it Take to Change a Lightbulb Act" that would phase out incandescent light bulbs by 2012 in favour of compact fluorescent bulbs.

According to the Federal Government, up to 95 per cent of the energy each standard light bulb uses is wasted, while compact fluorescents use only 20 per cent as much electricity to produce the same amount of light.

Energy Australia says by using just one 15-watt compact fluorescent bulb instead of a 75-watt standard bulb, consumers could save about $10 a year.

In Australia, lighting represents about 12 per cent of greenhouse gas emissions from households, about 25 per cent of commercial sector emissions, and a quarter of the emissions associated with public and street lighting.

The Federal Government estimates replacing the old bulbs with compact fluorescents in homes could cut greenhouse gas emissions by as much as 800,000 tonnes a year in 2008–12. Australia's emissions in 2004 totalled 564.7 million tonnes.

Mr Goldman said compact fluorescent bulbs were available that emitted a range of light.

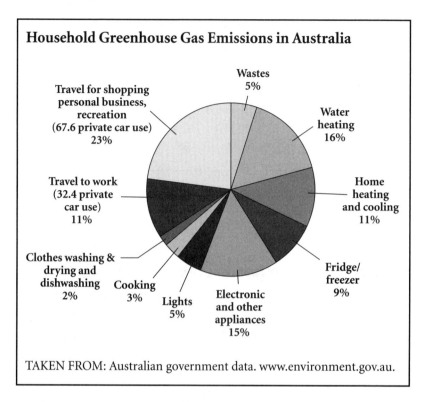

Household Greenhouse Gas Emissions in Australia

Wastes
5%

Travel for shopping
personal business,
recreation
(67.6 private car use)
23%

Water
heating
16%

Travel to work
(32.4 private
car use)
11%

Home
heating
and cooling
11%

Clothes washing &
drying and
dishwashing
2%

Cooking
3%

Lights
5%

Electronic
and other
appliances
15%

Fridge/
freezer
9%

TAKEN FROM: Australian government data. www.environment.gov.au.

"You can get warm white, which is a yellowish light, or natural, which is white, or day-light, which is more blueish."

The new bulbs would not necessarily require any rewiring of homes or offices, he said.

Greg Bourne, the chief executive of the conservation organisation WWF, said phasing out standard bulbs was a useful step in the transition to an energy-efficient world, but it passed on the cost directly to consumers.

"Architecturally, in some places it is difficult to change over," he said. "It [the federal decision] does feel like a knee-jerk reaction, but it is a step in the right direction."

The marketing director of Thorn Lighting Australia, Ian Wiseman, said he wanted to see government subsidies for importers and distributors.

It is understood there will be no ban on halogen lights, which are more efficient than the old bulbs.

A Big Switch

- Incandescent light bulbs were first developed almost 125 years ago.

- By 2005 about 100 million compact fluorescent light bulbs were sold in the US [United States], or about 5 per cent of the 2 billion light bulb market.

- Wal-Mart alone wants to sell 100 million CFLs [compact fluorescent light bulbs] by the end of this year.

- By using just one 15-watt compact fluorescent bulb instead of a 75-watt standard bulb, you can save about $10 a year on your energy bill.

- Compact fluorescent bulbs pay for themselves within 12 months.

Philippine Activists Protest Construction of a Coal-Fired Power Plant

Greenpeace

Hundreds of Filipino students are leading the call for local and national government officials to stop using coal. Jasper Inventor, of Greenpeace Southeast Asia, writes, "Filipinos have realized that climate change is a real threat to the country and are rejecting coal, one of the major contributors to global climate change." Instead, Filipinos are looking to renewable energy as an alternative to coal. According to Greenpeace, the Philippines' wind energy potential alone would be able to handle the country's total energy demand. Currently, however, clean technologies are not the foremost source in the Philippines' power mix.

Greenpeace is a global campaigning organization that acts to protect and conserve the environment and to promote peace.

As you read, consider the following questions:

1. What are some of the "better solutions" the people of the Philippines are considering for energy?
2. The wind energy potential in the Philippines is estimated to exceed the country's energy demand by how much?

Greenpeace, "Thousands Protest Against Planned Coal-Fired Power Plant in Iloilo," March 5, 2008. www.greenpeace.org. Reproduced by permission.

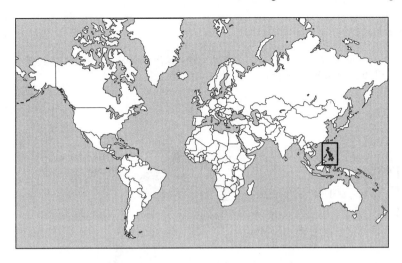

3. Clean technologies represent less than what percentage of the overall Philippine power mix?

Thousands joined an ecumenical prayer rally in Iloilo City [Philippines] today in protest against a proposed 164 MW [megawatt] coal-fired power plant, which if built would contribute to global climate change and lock the country in a dirty energy cycle for years to come.

Led by Catholic Bishops Council of Philippines (CBCP) President Archbishop Angel Lagdameo, the interfaith rally sends a strong signal to proponents of the coal-fired power plant they are not welcome in the city. Hundreds of students from St. Paul's University formed a 'QUIT COAL' sign to call on local and national government officials to reject coal.

Over the years, the residents of Iloilo and nearby Negros province have joined Greenpeace in urging for a switch to clean energy use in the country.

The Philippines is ranked number one on the global climate risk index in 2007 because the country is in a typhoon belt and many of the low-lying islands are under threat from

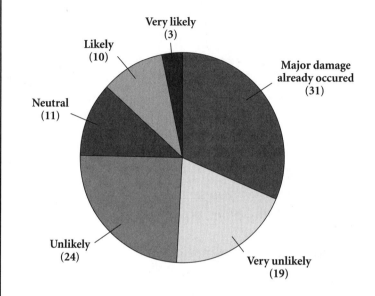

Experts are Pessimistic

Sustainability experts were asked if current progress on climate change will be enough to avert irreversible damage.

Very likely (3)

Likely (10)

Neutral (11)

Major damage already occured (31)

Unlikely (24)

Very unlikely (19)

TAKEN FROM: Globe Scan/World Business Council for Sustainable Development, 2007.

sea level rise. Coal-fired power plants account for 36% of the country's total CO_2 [carbon dioxide] emissions.

"Filipinos have realized that climate change is a real threat to the country and are rejecting coal, one of the major contributors to global climate change. People instead seek for better solutions offered by renewable energy from wind, sun or geothermal resources," said Jasper Inventor, Climate and Energy Campaigner of Greenpeace Southeast Asia.

On this exact day four years ago, the people of Iloilo rejected a proposed coal-fired power plat in Banate, a town approximately 40 kilometers from Iloilo City.

Other communities across the country have also rejected proposed coal-fired power plants. In 2002, Negros booted out a proposed coal-fired power plant and led to the declaration that the province becomes a model for 100% renewable energy development. In 2006, the Philippine National Oil Corporation stopped its coal-fired power plant project in Isabela after opposition from residents.

Over the years, the residents of Iloilo and nearby Negros province have joined Greenpeace in urging for a switch to clean energy use in the country. The Philippines' wind energy potential is estimated to meet seven times the country's total energy demand. However, clean technologies such as wind, solar and modern biomass represent less than 0.2% of the overall Philippine power mix in spite of promises from the Arroyo administration to reduce greenhouse gas emissions.

"Instead of harnessing the growing public opposition to climate damaging coal-fired power plants to help enable the shift towards greater use of renewable energy systems, the government sadly remains fixated on prolonging the country's deadly addiction to polluting energy plants. Climate change is far too great a risk for Filipinos that coal should altogether be phased out of the country's energy mix," Inventor concluded.

Periodical Bibliography

The following articles have been selected to supplement the diverse views presented in this chapter.

Decca Aitkenhead	"'Enjoy Life While You Can,'" *The Guardian*, March 1, 2008. www.guardian.co.uk.
BBC News	"How Can We Combat Climate Change?" June 10, 2005. http://news.bbc.co.uk.
David Cameron	"Change Our Political System and Our Lifestyles," *The Independent*, November 11, 2005.
Climate Action Network Europe	"What Can You Do About Climate Change?" 2007. www.climnet.org.
Rob Fenwick	"Sustainability: Act Now on Climate Change," *New Zealand Management*, April 3, 2006.
Green News Network	"Act Now on Climate Change: Go for Energy Efficiency," November 19, 2007. www.enn.com.
Bob Holmes	"US Struggling to Respond to Climate Shift," May 28, 2008. www.newscientist.com.
New Scientist	"Air Travel in the Tropics Causes More Warming," June 25, 2008.
Taking IT Global	"Climate Change: A Youth Guide to Action," November 2007. www.climate.takingitglobal. org.

For Further Discussion

Chapter 1

1. According to RoyalSociety.org and the Nobel Lecture of the Intergovernmental Panel on Climate Change, given by R.K. Pachauri, a significant majority of the world's climate scientists accept that human actions are changing the earth's climate. However, the viewpoints by Jeff Mason, Antony Barnett and Mark Townsend, and the U.S. House of Representatives Committee on Oversight and Government Relations all feature different groups that refute or oppose some aspects of climate change science. Who are these groups (e.g., researchers, companies, politicians, etc.)? What are their concerns? Are these concerns scientific or political?

2. Compare your answers (above) to the analysis of arguments advanced by climate change skeptics presented by Fred Pearce. How is debating the processes, timelines, or possible effects of human-induced climate change different from debating the existence of human-induced climate change?

Chapter 2

1. Compare and contrast the discussion of possible regional effects of climate change in the viewpoint by Michael Case with the viewpoints by Singy Hanyona, the United Nations Office for the Coordination of Humanitarian Affairs, and Fred de Sam Lazaro. Do the viewpoints focus on the possible effects of climate change on nature or humans? How do the viewpoints suggest that environmental and human concerns are closely related?

2. Many sources in this chapter focus on climate change's affect on human life, culture, economy, and human-made environments such as cities. Which issues do you think are most important? Which issues do you think currently receive the most attention? Why?

Chapter 3

1. According to the viewpoint by Rachel Oliver, how are climate change issues related to human rights and equity?

2. Using the arguments advanced in this chapter, discuss how you think the problem of emissions in developing nations should be addressed. Should developing nations be responsible for their own emissions or should they be permitted to develop without addressing environmental concerns? Should wealthier nations provide aid for "green" development?

Chapter 4

1. Opinion is the expression of a person's thoughts or his or her evaluation of a subject. Which viewpoints in this chapter feature opinion? What words helped you identify opinion? How does opinion differ from factual reporting?

2. Bias is a preference for a particular viewpoint or the presentation of one viewpoint at the expense of contradicting another. What sources in this chapter contain bias? What words help identify bias? How does bias differ from opinion?

Glossary

Adaptation The process of change in living organisms to better conform with environmental conditions or other external stimuli.

Annex A A list of the six greenhouse gases covered under the Kyoto Protocol, including carbon dioxide (CO_2), methane (CH_4), nitrous oxide (N_2O), hydrofluorocarbons (HFCs), perfluorocarbons (PFCs), and sulpher hexafloride (SF_6); also called the "Basket of Gases."

Annex I parties The list of industrialized countries that have agreed under the United Nations Framework Convention on Climate Change to reduce their greenhouse gas emissions to target levels below their 1990 emissions levels.

Anthropogenic Produced or influenced by human activity

Arctic melting The melting of the ice sheet of the Arctic Ocean, usually used to refer to accelerated melting caused by climate change.

Biodiversity The variety of organisms found within a specified geographic region.

Carbon dioxide (CO_2) A colorless, odorless, gas that is part of air. Increased levels of anthropogenic CO_2 in the atmosphere are a major contributor to global climate change.

Carbon sinks Processes that absorb more carbon dioxide from the atmosphere than they release. Both the oceans and terrestrial biosphere can act as carbon sinks.

Carbon tax A tax levied on the carbon content of oil, coal, and natural gas to discourage the use of fossil fuels and reduce carbon dioxide emissions.

Chlorofluorocarbons (CFCs) CFCs are synthetic industrial gases composed of chlorine, fluorine, and carbon. CFCs may be used as refrigerants, aerosol propellants, cleaning solvents, and in the manufacture of plastic foam. CFCs deplete the ozone layer and contribute to global warming.

Clean Development Mechanism (CDM) One of the three market mechanisms established by the Kyoto Protocol to promote sustainable development. The CDM grants greenhouse gas emissions credits to industrialized countries that invest in emission reduction projects in developing countries.

Climate The long-term average weather of a region including typical weather patterns, heat waves, cold spells, and the frequency and intensity of storms. Climate is not the same as weather.

Climate change Refers to changes in long-term trends in the average climate, such as changes in average temperatures, rainfall, etc.

Climate justice A social, political, and environmental movement that stresses the right of all people to live free from the negative consequences of global climate change.

Developing country A country that is in the process of industrializing.

Ecosystem A community of organisms and the physical environment in which they live.

Emissions The release of substances (e.g., greenhouse gases) into the atmosphere.

Emissions cap A mandated limit on the total amount of anthropogenic greenhouse gas emissions that can be released into the atmosphere. This can be measured as gross emissions or as net emissions (emissions minus gases that are "captured").

Emissions trading A market mechanism that allows emitters of greenhouse gases—including nations and companies—to buy, sell, or trade the right to emit a certain volume of greenhouse gases into the atmosphere.

Environmental degradation The process of depleting or destroying a renewable resource such as soil, forests, pasture, or wildlife by using it at a faster rate than it can be naturally replenished.

Famine Widespread shortage of food that is usually accompanied by malnutrition, starvation, epidemic, and increased mortality.

Food scarcity An inadequate supply of food to meet the nutritional needs of people within a certain area.

Fossil fuel A carbon-based fuel formed from the remains of once-living organisms, including coal, oil, and natural gas.

GDP (Gross domestic product) Gross domestic product, a measure of overall economic activity.

Global North Countries located in the Northern Hemisphere (Europe, North America, and Asia), usually used to refer to such countries as being highly industrialized or developed.

Global South Countries located in the Southern Hemisphere (South America and Africa).

Global warming The progressive gradual rise of Earth's average surface temperature thought to be caused in part by an anthropogenic increase in concentrations of greenhouse gases (GHGs) in the atmosphere.

Great Ocean Conveyor Large-scale ocean circulation that carries warm water to some parts of the world and cold water to other parts. These circulating ocean currents have a major impact on the global climate.

Greenhouse effect The insulating effect of atmospheric greenhouse gases (e.g., water vapor, carbon dioxide, methane, etc.) that warms Earth's temperature.

Greenhouse gas (GHG) Any gas that contributes to the "greenhouse effect" by absorbing infrared radiation in the atmosphere. GHGs include carbon dioxide, water vapor, and methane.

Inundation (flooding) The overflowing of a river or body of water so that it covers normally dry land; often used to denote a more permanent event than flooding.

Intergovernmental Panel on Climate Change (IPCC) A United Nations organization established in 1988 to work with the World Meteorological Organization and the UN Environment Programme. The IPCC is responsible for providing the scientific and technical foundation for the United Nations Framework Convention on Climate Change (UNFCC), primarily through the publication of periodic assessment reports.

Kyoto Protocol An international agreement adopted in December 1997 in Kyoto, Japan. The Protocol sets binding emission targets for developed countries that would reduce their emissions an average 5.2 percent below 1990 levels.

Montreal Protocol (on Substances That Deplete the Ozone Layer): An international agreement to phase out the use of ozone-depleting compounds such as methyl chloroform, carbon tetrachloride, and CFCs.

Rain forest A large, dense forest in a hot, humid region, characterized by an abundance of diverse plant and animal life.

Recycling Collecting and processing solid waste products to make new products.

Renewable Energy Energy obtained from sources that can produce indefinitely without depletion, including geothermal, wind, solar, and biomass energy.

Salinization Process whereby the salt content of soil or freshwater gradually accumulates to above normal levels, typically through the evaporation of standing water.

Sea level rise A change in the average global sea level brought about by volume changes in the world ocean.

Sequestration The removal of atmospheric carbon dioxide, either through biological processes (e.g. plants and trees) or geological processes, such as the storage of carbon dioxide in underground reservoirs.

Vector-borne disease Disease that results from an infection transmitted to humans and other animals by blood-feeding anthropods, such as mosquitoes, ticks, and fleas. Examples of vector-borne diseases include Dengue fever, viral encephalitis, Lyme disease, and malaria.

Weather Describes the short-term (i.e., hourly and daily) state of the atmosphere. Weather is not the same as climate.

Organizations to Contact

The editors have compiled the following list of organizations concerned with the issues debated in this book. The descriptions are derived from materials provided by the organizations. All have publications or information available for interested readers. The list was compiled on the date of publication of the present volume; the information provided here may change. Be aware that many organizations take several weeks or longer to respond to inquiries, so allow as much time as possible.

Climate Institute
1785 Massachusetts Avenue NW, Washington, DC 20036
(202) 547-0104 • Fax: (202) 547-0111
E-mail: info@climate.org
Web site: www.climate.org

The Climate Institute seeks to inform key decision makers, heighten international awareness of climate change, and identify practical ways of achieving reductions in greenhouse gas emissions. The Climate Institute achieves these goals through symposia, conferences, roundtable discussions, and special briefings that bring together government, business, and civic leaders.

Environmental Justice and Climate Change Initiative
1326 Fourteenth Street NW, Washington, DC 20005
(202) 234-9665 • Fax: (901) 234-9665
Web site: www.ejcc.org.

The Environmental Justice and Climate Change Initiative is a group of American environmental justice, climate justice, religious, policy, and advocacy networks that work together to promote climate policy. The group's mission is to educate and engage the people of North America toward the creation and implementation of domestic and international climate policies. Publications available at the Web site include "10 Principles for Just Climate Change Policy in the U.S."

Greenpeace International

Ottho Heldringstraat 5, Amsterdam   1066 AZ
The Netherlands
20 7182000 • Fax: 20 5148151
E-mail: supporter.services@int.greenpeace.org
Web site: www.greenpeace.org

Founded in Canada in 1971, Greenpeace is one of the largest environmental groups in the world with twenty-eight national and regional offices. Greenpeace uses volunteer activism to address environmental issues such as global climate change, whaling, deforestation, nuclear power, and clean energy production.

Intergovernmental Panel on Climate Change (IPCC)

Phone: +41-22-730-8208/84
E-mail: IPCC-Sec@wmo.int
Web site: www.ipcc.ch

The Intergovernmental Panel on Climate Change (IPCC) is a scientific body dedicated to evaluating the risk of global climate change. The IPCC comprehensively and objectively examines the latest scientific information to provide decision makers and others interested in climate change with an objective source of information. Two organizations of the United Nations, the United Nations Environment Programme (UNEP) and the World Meteorological Organization (WMO), founded the IPCC in 1988. IPCC reports are available on its Web site.

National Climatic Data Center (NCDC)

Federal Building, Asheville, NC   28801
(828) 271-4800 • Fax: (828) 271-4876
Web site: www.ncdc.noaa.gov

The National Climatic Data Center (NCDC) is the world's largest active archive of weather data. NCDC produces climate publications and provides climate data to researchers. NCDC operates the World Data Center for Meteorology, which is located at NCDC in Asheville, North Carolina, and the World Data Center for Paleoclimatology in Boulder, Colorado. The Web site provides climate change graphs and maps.

Pew Center on Global Climate Change
2101 Wilson Boulevard, Suite 550, Arlington, VA   22201
(703) 516-4146 • Fax: (703) 841-1422
Web site: www.pewclimate.org

The Pew Center on Global Climate Change brings together business leaders, policy makers, scientists, and other experts to reduce greenhouse gas emissions and combat global climate change. Pew Charitable Trusts provides funding for the Pew Center on Global Climate Change. Facts, graphs, and figures on global climate change are available on its Web site.

World Wildlife Fund (WWF)
Av. du Mont-Blanc 1196, Gland
   Switzerland
Web site: www.panda.org

The World Wildlife Fund (WWF) is an international nongovernmental organization dedicated to conservation of the natural environment. The WWF typically works with local nonprofit organizations to perform conservation work within a specific area. Currently, the WWF conducts more than 1300 conservation projects around the world.

Bibliography of Books

Richard B. Alley   *The Two-Mile Time Machine: Ice Cores, Abrupt Climate Change, and Our Future.* Princeton, NJ: Princeton University Press, 2002.

Martin Beniston   *Climatic Change: Implications for the Hydrological Cycle and for Water Management.* Boston, MA: Kluwer Academic Publishers, 2002.

Wallace S. Broecker and Robert Kunzig   *Fixing Climate: What Past Climate Changes Reveal About the Current Threat—and How to Counter It.* New York: Three Books Publishing, 2008.

Neville G. Brown   *History of Climate Change.* London, UK: Routledge, 2001.

Andrew E. Dessler and Edward A. Parson   *The Science and Politics of Global Climate Change: A Guide to the Debate.* New York: Cambridge University Press, 2006.

Joseph F.C. DiMento and Pamela M. Doughman   *Climate Change: What It Means for Us, Our Children, and Our Grandchildren (American and Comparative Environmental Policy).* Boston, MA: Massachusetts Institute of Technology, 2007.

Kerry Emanuel, Judith A. Layzer, and William R. Moomaw   *What We Know About Climate Change.* Cambridge, MA: Boston Review Books, 2007.

Brian Fagan	*Floods, Famines, and Emperors: El Nino and the Fate of Civilizations.* New York: Basic Books, 2000.
Michael B. Gerrard	*Global Climate Change and U.S. Law.* Chicago, IL: American Bar Association, 2007.
Dinyar Godrej	*The No-Nonsense Guide to Climate Change.* Oxford, UK: New Internationalist Publications, 2001.
Paul G. Harris	*Europe and Global Climate Change: Politics, Foreign Policy and Regional Cooperation.* Cheltenham, UK: Edward Elgar Publishing Limited, 2007.
Elizabeth Kolbert	*Field Notes from a Catastrophe: Man, Nature, and Climate Change.* New York: Bloomsbury Publishing, 2006.
Bjørn Lomborg	*Cool It: The Skeptical Environmentalist's Guide to Global Warming.* New York: Knopf, 2007.
Thomas E. Lovejoy and Lee Hannah	*Climate Change and Biodiversity.* Grand Rapids, MI: Sheridan Books, 2005.
Urs Luterbacher and Detlef F. Sprinz	*International Relations and Global Climate Change (Global Environmental Accord: Strategies for Sustainability and Institutional Innovation).* Boston, MA: Massachusetts Institute of Technology, 2001.

Roderick J. McIntosh

The Way the Wind Blows: Climate, History, and Human Action. New York: Columbia University Press, 2000.

Robert Mendelsohn and James E. Neumann

The Impact of Climate Change on the United States Economy. New York: Cambridge University Press, 1999.

Susanne C. Moser and Lisa Dilling

Creating a Climate for Change: Communicating Climate Change and Facilitating Social Change. Cambridge: Cambridge University Press, 2007.

Patrick D. Nunn

Environmental Change in the Pacific Basin: Chronologies, Causes, Consequences. New York: Wiley, 1999.

Michael E. Schlesinger, Haroon S. Kheshgi, Joel Smith, Francisco C. de la Chesnaye, John M. Reilly, Tom Wilson, and Charles Kolstad

Human-Induced Climate Change: An Interdisciplinary Assessment. Cambridge, UK: Cambridge University Press, 2007.

Roy Spence

Climate Confusion: How Global Warming Hysteria Leads to Bad Science, Pandering Politicians and Misguided Policies That Hurt the Poor. New York: Encounter Books, 2008.

Robert Strom

Hot House: Global Climate Change and the Human Condition. New York: Copernicus Books, 2007.

Michael A. Toman, Ujjayant Chakravorty, and Shreekant Gupta	*India and Global Climate Change: Perspectives on Economics and Policy from a Developing Country.* Washington, DC: RFF Press, 2003.
Maurice Van Arsdol Jr.	*Impacts of Global Sea Level Rise on California Coastal Population Resources: Population, Environment, Development Interactions.* Los Angeles: University of Southern California, 2003.
Robert T. Watson	*The Regional Impacts of Climate Change: An Assessment of Vulnerability.* Cambridge, UK: Cambridge University Press, 1998.

Index

Geographic headings and page numbers in **boldface** refer to viewpoints about that country or region.

A

Acid rain, 47, 172–173, 177
Adaptation, society, 36–39, 78, 88–89, 106
Adaptive capacity, 34–35, 87, 169
Aerosols, 15, 38, 47
Africa, 32, 83–89, 91
Agriculture, 162–163
    Africa, 32, 83–86, 87, 89
    Amazon basin, 119–122
    Bangladesh, 98, 101–102
    China, 174–175
    deforestation, 183, 189–190
    Middle East, 91, 92
Aid
    agricultural, 83–86, 89
    disaster relief, 97–98
Air pollution, 79, 122–123, 170, 173, 175, 177, 178
Air Trends Report (EPA), 71
Allergenic plants, 123
Amazon River basin, 109–124
American Geophysical Union, 58
American Petroleum Institute, 68
Animals
    arctic, 70, 137, 138, 139–140
    forest, 109, 116, 117, 119, 188, 189
Antarctic ice, 39
Arctic changes, 70, 135–139
Arctic Climate Impact Assessment, 135, 137, 142
Arrhenius, Svante, 60

Asia, regional impacts, 100, 154
    See also specific countries
Australia, 199–203
    citizens' carbon footprints, 156, 201, 202
    light bulb policy, 199–203

B

Bali conference, 2007, 55, 56, 58, 59, 61, 116, 160
Ban Ki-moon, 57, 59
Bangladesh, 96–102, 154
Barnett, Antony, 62–66
Barrier project, Venice, 144–149
Basic needs/resources, 31–32, 75, 76, 92, 172
Becker, Markus, 55–61
Benefits
    climate change offering, 62–66, 167
    greenhouse gases, 21, 43, 60
Besser, Linton, 199–203
Billion Tree Program (UN), 183–192
Binding emissions reduction plans, 16–17, 57, 59
    harm developing nations, 165–169
    verbiage changes, 58
Biodiversity
    Amazon basin, 110, 113, 114, 116, 117–118
    forests, 184, 188–189
    threats, 33, 86
Blair, Tony, 64–65

Brandt, Willy, 39–40
Brazil, 120, 121
Bronze Age, 30
Bush, George W.
  administration's science manipulation, 61, 67–72
  international non-
  cooperation, 56, 58, 63, 64,
  137, 166
Butler, Rhett, 116

C

Californian leadership, 82, 201
Canada, 135–143
Carbon capture. *See* Offsetting
  emissions
Carbon dioxide, atmospheric, 21,
  22, 43–44, 161–162
  Amazon basin, 112, 115, 120,
  121
  climate sensitivity, 168
  geographic attribution, 163
  See also Greenhouse gases;
  Offsetting emissions; Reduc-
  tion, greenhouse gases
Carbon footprints, 163, 187, 196
  Australia, 156, 201, 202
  China, 176
  Dell Computer, 198
  rich vs. poor nations, 153
Carbon Monitoring for Action
  (CARMA) database, 161
Carbon offsetting, 81, 102, 195
Care International Zambia, 85–86
Carrera, Fabio, 144–145, 149
Case, Michael, 109–124
Censorship, scientific reports, 67,
  69–71
Center for Global Development
  (CGD), 160–164

Center for International Climate
  and Environmental Research
  (CICERO), 165
Center for International Environ-
  mental Law, 139
CEQ. *See* White House Council on
  Environmental Quality (CEQ)
Chemical pollutants, 139–140, 175
China, 170–180
  greenhouse gas production/
  responsibility, 57, 58, 61, 82,
  161, 163, 170–180
  warfare, history, 30
Chlorofluorocarbons (CFCs), 15
Climate cycles, 48
Clouds, 46–47
Coal, 81
  China, 178–179, 180
  Philippines, 204–207
Coastline changes. *See* Sea level
  rises
Collective scientific endeavor, 20–
  25, 29
Companies' stewardship, 193–198
Competitive Enterprise Institute,
  141–142
Computer recycling, 195
Conflict, resource-based, 30–32,
  92, 172
Connaughton, James, 57, 61,
  71–72
Consensus. *See* Scientific commu-
  nity consensus
Consumer class, 157–158
Cooney, Philip, 69, 71
Copenhagen conference, 2009, 57,
  61
Coral reefs, 103, 104
Costs, environmental improve-
  ment, 167
  greenhouse gas reduction, 37,
  59, 76

vs. inaction impacts, 37–39, 76–82

light bulb changes, 200–201, 203

Crichton, Michael, 42

Crisis aversion, opinions, 206

Criticisms, climate change. *See* Skepticism

Currents, oceans, 47

Customer relationships, 194–195

Cycles, solar, 45

Cyclone Sidr (2007), 96, 97–98

D

Dambeck, Holger, 55–61

de Sam Lazaro, Fred, 96–102

Deaths

Chinese pollution-attributed, 173–174

global, and climate change, 94, 122, 154

hunger, 93

mining, 178

water-related, 97–98, 100

Deforestation

agriculture, 183, 189–190

effects, 111, 113–115, 116, 162, 189

primary forests, 188

Degradation, environmental

China, 171–175

economic status and, 154, 155

historical, 30

Dell, Michael, 193–198

Dell Computer, 193–198

Demand, energy, Energy consumption

Denials. *See* Skepticism

Desertification, 154, 174, 184, 188

Developing nations' responsibilities, 16–17, 25, 58, 80, 159–164

See also Poor societies; specific nations

Disagreements, scientific community, 41–49

Disasters. *See* Extreme weather; Natural disasters

Disease, 122, 154

See also Health issues

Disinformation

Bush administration, 61, 67–72

ExxonMobil, 53, 66

Dobriansky, Paula, 56–57

Dominant paradigm, 49–50

Droughts, 83, 86–87, 88–89, 114–115

E

Earthjustice, 137

Ecological footprints, 196

See also Carbon footprints

Economic costs. *See* Costs

Economic development

China, 17, 170–180

deemed at odds with emissions reduction, 16–17, 59, 64–65, 180

India, 17, 157

not at odds with emissions reduction, 36, 80, 194–198

Economic disparities

China, 171

climate change's effects and, 24, 30–31, 39, 78, 91, 152–158

emissions ownership and, 78, 80, 88, 153, 159–164

The Economist, 170–180

Ecosystems, threats, 23, 33

Amazon basin, 112, 115, 116, 117–119

islands, 103, 104–105

Egypt, 92
Eilperin, Juliet, 70
El Niño/Southern Oscillation, 111–112, 114–115, 122
Emissions reductions. *See* Reduction, greenhouse gases
Energy consumption
    China, 170, 171–173, 175–180
    corporate responsibility, 193–198
    everyday reductions, 185, 196
    Philippines, 204, 207
    world rates, 22, 194
Energy efficiency, 81, 175, 178
    business products, 195, 196–197
    light bulbs, 199–203
Environmental injustice, 154–155
    See also Economic disparities
Environmental Protection Agency (EPA), 69, 71–72
EPA. *See* Environmental Protection Agency (EPA)
EPA, Massachusetts v. (2007), 72
Erosion
    coastline, 99, 105, 107, 154
    land, 113
    prevention, 184, 191
    See also Desertification; Land loss; Reforestation
Esso. *See* ExxonMobil
EU. *See* European Union
European Union, 55–61
    condemning U.S. policies, 55–61
    pledges/action, 16–17, 52
Extinction risks, 33
Extreme weather, 23, 36, 66, 78
    Cyclone Sidr, 96, 97–98
    drought, 83, 86–87, 88–89, 114–115

flooding, 98–101, 112, 122, 154
    health and, 122–123
    hurricanes, 69–70, 71
    predicted, 118–119, 174
ExxonMobil, 53, 64, 66

F

Farming. *See* Agriculture; Forestry farming
Federal interference, U.S., 61, 67–72
Feedback effects, 46–49, 113, 115, 162
Fires, 114, 115, 122–123
Fishes, 117–119, 123
Floating buildings, 100–101
Floodgates, Venice, 144–149
Flooding, 98–101, 112, 122, 154
Fluorescent light bulbs, 199–203
Food and Agriculture Organization, UN, 91
Food chain, 139–140
Food prices, 91–95
Food security, 32, 83–89, 90–95
Forestry farming, 119, 120–121, 162, 190
Forests
    destruction, 111, 113–115, 116
    mangroves, 104, 123
    reforestation, 183–187, 190–192, 197–198
    roles, 112, 188–189, 191–192
    safeguarding, 116, 195
Fossil fuels
    China, 171–173, 176, 177, 178–179
    Philippines, 204–207
    usage rates, 22, 81, 162, 166
Framework Convention on Climate Change, 82, 84–85, 166

Free market approaches. *See* Market approaches
Fresh water. *See* Water resources
Frew, Wendy, 199–203
Fuel costs, 176, 179
Fuel economy, 175–176
Funding, research
    corporate interests and, 53, 64, 66, 167
    skeptics' challenges, 51–54

G

G8 nations, 24–25, 64
    See also Rich nations
Gertz, Emily, 135–143
Glaciers, 32, 99, 154, 174
"Global" climate change, 16
Global Environment Facility (GEF), 89
Global South. *See* Poor societies
Global warming, 88
    editing of reports, 71
    IPCC findings, 15–16, 28, 33, 34, 35–36, 38, 174
    public opinion polls, 65, 79
    See also Temperatures
Goldberg, Don, 137, 138–139, 141–142
Gore, Al
    An Inconvenient Truth, 161
    Nobel Peace Prize, 2007, 26, 27, 34
    reaction, Bush administration non-action, 58
Green companies, 193–198
Greenhouse effect, 43–44, 46, 48
    initial naming, 14
    reported as positive, 62–66, 166–169
    theory introduction, 60

Greenhouse gases
    benefits, 21, 43, 60
    deforestation influence, 113–115, 116
    harmful effects, 21, 22–23
    regulations, court cases, 71–72
    sources by sector and region, 157, 163, 176, 187, 202
    UN resolution, 1988, 28
    See also Developing nations' responsibilities; Energy efficiency; Reduction, greenhouse gases; Rich nations; specific nations
Greenland, 35, 39
Greenpeace, 65–66, 204–207
Gronas, Sigbjorn, 165–169
Gross domestic product
    climate change costs eroding, 76
    gas levels stabilization compared, 79
    "green" GDP, China, 179–180
Group of 8, 24–25, 64

H

Haag, Amanda Leigh, 106
Hanyona, Singy, 83–89
Hardware, 196–197
Health issues
    air pollution and, 173–174
    Amazon region, 122–123
    diseases, 122, 154
    Inuit people, 140
    water resources and, 32–33, 105, 122, 146–148, 173–174
Heger, Monica, 53
Historical climate change studies, 14–15, 23, 48, 110–111
History, world, 30
House of Representatives, Oversight and Government Reform Committee, 61, 67–72

Human rights, 137–139, 141–142
Hunger
    Africa, 83–87, 93
    Middle East, 92–95
Hurricanes, 69–70, 71

I

ICC. *See* Inuit Circumpolar Conference (ICC)
Ice melts
    Arctic habitat, 136, 137–138
    fresh water impacts, 32, 154, 174
    vapor/cloud impacts, 46–47
    water levels impacts, 23–24, 35, 99
The Impacts of Climate Change: An Appraisal of the Future (International Policy Network), 62–64, 167–169
Incandescent bulbs, 199–203
An Inconvenient Truth (film), 161
India
    ancient history, 29
    economic growth, 157
    greenhouse gas production/responsibility, 58, 61, 163
Individual consumption levels, 153, 154–158, 163
Indonesian conference. *See* Bali conference, 2007
Infectious diseases, 122
Information technology companies, 193–198
Infrared radiation, 43–44
Inter-American Commission on Human Rights, 137, 141
Intergovernmental Panel on Climate Change (IPCC), 15–16
    China notes, 174
    data contested, 167–168

Fourth Assessment Report, 27–28, 31–35, 37, 39
ice melt data, 23–24, 46–47, 139
influence, 51, 52–53, 161
Nobel Peace Prize lecture, 2007, 26–40
rising sea levels, 35, 103–108, 123, 146
surface temperature data, 21, 46
International agreements, 16–17, 82, 165, 166
    See also specific agreements
International Policy Network (IPN) (UK), 62–66, 166–169
Inuit Circumpolar Conference (ICC), 136–139, 140–143
Inuit peoples, 135–143
Inventor, Jasper, 204, 206, 207
IPCC. *See* Intergovernmental Panel on Climate Change (IPCC)
Islamic Relief, 97
Islands' vulnerability, 33, 35, 38, 103–108, 205–206
Italy, 144–149

J

Jaffe, Eric, 144–149
Joint statement on climate change, 20–25
Justice, environmental, 154–155

K

Karl, Thomas, 70–71
Kempthorne, Dirk, 70
Kerry, John, 14
King, David, 42, 64
Kyoto Protocol (1997), 15, 42, 82, 160
    extending, 53

international participation, 167
Inuit human rights petition, 138
rejection/criticisms, 65, 72, 168
term expiration, 56

L

La Niña, 112
Laborde, Kent, 69
Land loss
  Arctic, 35, 136, 138
  Bangladesh, 99–102
  China, 174
  islands, 103–108
  Venice, 144–149
Leadership. *See* Responsibility, political
Lebanon, 93
Legal challenges, 137, 138–139, 141–142
Light bulb evolution, 199–203
Lindzen, Richard, 48–49
Literature, scientific. *See* Scientific community consensus; Scientific reports
Little Ice Age, 48
Lomborg, Bjorn, 66, 169
Low-carbon technology, 80, 81, 102, 177, 204, 207

M

Maathai, Wangari, 184–185, 185–186
Malawi, 83–89
Maldives, 38
Mangroves, 104, 123
Marburger, John, 58–59
Market approaches, 81, 165, 166–167, 168–169, 197

Mason, Jeff, 51–54
Massachusetts v. EPA (2007), 72
Mauna Loa observatory, 43
Maya civilization, 30
Measures of change, 21
Media coverage
  Arctic warming, 137
  manipulation, 67, 69–72
  ozone layer, 15
Medieval Warm Period, 48
Meltwater. *See* Ice melts
Middle East, 90–95
Migration, human, 35, 102, 106, 108
Modeling, predictions
  Amazon basin, 112, 113–114, 118–119, 121–122
  global effects, 46–48, 77–78
  questioned, 54
Montreal Protocol (1987), 15
Morris, Julian, 64, 66
Mortality rates. *See* Deaths
MOSE system (Venice), 144–149
Mozambique, 87, 89

N

National Academy of Science, opinions, 72
National Adaptation Programme of Action on Climate Change (NAPA), 85
National Climatic Data Center, 70–71
Natural disasters, 54, 107, 154
  See also Extreme weather
Near East. *See* Middle East
La Niña, 112
El Niño/Southern Oscillation, 111–112, 114–115, 122
Nobel Chemistry Prize, 60
Nobel Committee, 28–29

Nobel Peace Prize
  1971 (Brandt), 39–40
  2007 (IPCC/Gore), 26–29
Non-energy emissions, 81, 113–114, 162, 189
North-South disparities. *See* Economic disparities
Nuclear power, 177

O

Ocean/freshwater warming, 23–24, 47, 104, 117–118
  See also Sea level rises
Offices, energy cuts, 193, 195, 196–197
Offsetting emissions
  carbon credits, 81, 102, 195
  trees, 162, 183–187, 190–192, 197–198
Oil industry, 68–69
  ExxonMobil, 53, 64, 66
  world routes, 172
Oliver, Rachel, 152–158
Oman, 94–95
Organic pollutants, 139–140
Ozone layer, 15

P

Pachauri, R.K., 26–40
Paradigm problem, 49–50
Pearce, Fred, 41–50
Philippines, 204–207
Plant a Tree for Me Program (Dell), 197–198
Plant for the Planet Program (UN), 183–192
Plant species. *See* Biodiversity
Plantation forestry, 119–121, 162, 190
Plants, 48, 118, 123
  See also Biodiversity; Forests

Polar bears, 70, 137, 138
Polar ice. *See* Ice melts
Policy. *See* Responsibility, political; White House executive policy
Pollution
  acid rain, 47, 172–173, 177
  air, 79, 122–123, 170, 173, 175, 177, 178
  chemicals, 139–140, 175
  poverty and, 155
  sewage, 146–148, 173
Poor societies
  developing nations' responsibilities, 16–17, 25, 58, 80, 159–164
  disproportionately affected, 24, 30–31, 39, 78, 91, 152–158
  emissions production, 78, 88, 153
  harmed by emissions restrictions, 169
  See also Rich nations
Population migration, 35, 102, 106, 108
Positive/negative feedbacks, 46–49, 113, 115, 162
Power use. *See* Energy consumption
Pre-industrial atmospheric levels
  goal, 37, 57–58
  today's levels vs., 21, 43, 45, 77
Precipitation
  Amazon basin, 111–112, 113, 116, 118, 119–120, 121
  snow cover levels, 139
Predictions
  crisis aversion chances, 206
  energy demand, 22, 194
  extreme weather, 118–119, 174

temperature increase results, 35–36, 46–48, 77–78, 112–113
temperature increase statistics, 16, 21, 33, 45, 46, 47, 77, 88, 112
See also Modeling, predictions; Sea level rises
Pricing, carbon, 81
Primary forests, 188
Product lifecycles, 194, 195–197
Protests, 92–93, 175, 204, 205
Public opinion, global warning, 65

Q

Quantifiable targets, 58
See also Binding emissions reduction plans

R

Rahman, Atiq, 99, 102
Rainfall patterns
Amazon basin, 111–112, 113, 116, 118, 119–120, 121
decreases, effects, 35
islands, 105
Rainforest. *See* Amazon River basin; Forests
Recycling and recycled materials, 195
REDD (Reducing Emissions from Deforestation and Degradation), 116
Reduction, greenhouse gases, 22, 36–38, 52, 78–80, 82
companies, 193–198
mandatory/binding plans, 16–17, 57–59
market-driven methods, 81, 165, 168–169
poor vs. rich nations, 160–162, 164

stabilization level, 37, 78–79, 81
technology-enabled, 80, 81, 102, 177, 199–203
See also Non-energy emissions
Reforestation, 162, 183–187, 190–192, 197–198
Refugees, 102, 154
Renewable energy, 177, 198, 204, 207
Report on the Environment (EPA), 71
Reports. *See* Historical climate change studies; Scientific reports
Resettlement, populations, 102, 106, 108
Resources. *See* Basic needs/resources
Responsibility, political, 80, 166, 167
Australia, 201
California, 82, 201
China, 82, 179–180
EU, 16–17, 52, 82
G8 nations, 24–25
United States, 55–61, 136–137, 166
See also White House executive policy
Restrictions, international. *See* Binding emissions reduction plans
Rezwan, Mohammad, 100–101
Rich nations
debt to poor nations, 154–155
emissions production, 58, 88, 136–137, 152, 153, 155–158, 163
emissions reduction responsibilities, 16–17, 55–61, 80, 136–137, 141, 164
See also Poor societies
Rivers. *See* Amazon River basin; Water resources

Rizvi, Haider, 159–164
RoyalSociety.org, 20–25
Russia, 138

S

Scientific community consensus,
41–50
joint statement on climate
change, 20–25
skeptics' challenges, 51–54
Scientific reports
censorship/editing, 67, 69–71
need for more, 39
See also Historical climate
change studies
Sea level rises, 23–24, 123–124,
147
Asia, 100
Bangladesh, 98–99
China, 174
islands' vulnerability, 33, 35,
38, 103–108, 205–206
myth, 63
Venice, 144–149
Security
basic components, 31
displacement and, 35
food, 32, 83–89, 90–95
IPCC concerns, 29, 30, 31,
39–40
Seip, Hans Martin, 165–169
Sensitivity, geographic regions,
33–34
Severe weather. *See* Extreme
weather
Sewage, 146–148, 173
Skepticism, 42–43, 44–45, 48–50
China, 179–180
funding cuts and research
challenges, 51–54
institutes, 62–64, 141–142,
166–169

Snow cover levels, 139
Solar cycles, 45
Sources, greenhouse gas emissions,
157, 163, 176, 187, 202
South Africa, 88
South America, 109–134
Species. *See* Biodiversity
Stabilization. *See* Reduction,
greenhouse gases
Stampf, Olaf, 60
State Environmental Protection
Administration (SEPA) (China),
174, 177, 179–180
Steiner, Achim, 184, 185
Stern, Nicholas, 75–82
The Stern Review Report, 75–82
Stockholm Convention, 140
*Strategic Plan of the Climate
Change Science Program*, 71
Subsidence farming, 119–120
Subsidies, 92, 94–95, 175–176

T

Technology improvements, 80, 81,
102, 177, 204, 207
Temperatures
history, charted, 23, 44–45, 48,
110–111
increase prediction statistics,
16, 21, 33, 45, 46, 47, 77, 88,
112
increase results prediction,
35–36, 46–48, 77–78, 112–
113
increases and agriculture,
119–120, 162–163, 174–175
increases and extreme
weather, 118–119, 174
water warming, 23–24, 47,
104, 117–118
Testimony, editing, 69, 70–71

Tides, 145
  See also Sea level rises
Tourism, 106–107, 148
Townsend, Mark, 62–66
Traditional farming, 83, 87
Treaties. *See* International agreements
Trees. *See* Forestry farming; Forests; Reforestation
Tropical islands, 103–108
Tuvalu, 106

U

United Kingdom, 62–66
  carbon impacts, 153, 163
  emissions reduction goals, 166
  International Policy Network opinions, 62–66, 166–169
United Nations
  Environment Programme (UNEP), 27, 155, 183–192
  Food and Agriculture Organization (FAO), 91
  Framework Convention on Climate Change (UNFCCC), 82, 84–85, 166
  General Assembly, 28, 38
  Office for the Coordination of Humanitarian Affairs, 90–95
  World Food Programme, 93
  See also Intergovernmental Panel on Climate Change (IPCC); Kyoto Protocol (1997)
United States, 67–72
  Bush White House science interference, 61, 67–72
  climate policy and rainforests, 116
  condemnation by other nations, 55–61, 136–137, 141
  greenhouse gas production, 57, 59, 88, 136–137, 153, 163

non-cooperation, international treaties, 16–17, 57–59, 61, 138, 166
  policy hearings, 68, 142
United States Agency for International Development (USAID), 88
U.S. House of Representatives. *See* House of Representatives

V

Venice, 144–149
Volcanic eruptions, 45, 107
Voluntary approach, emissions, 16–17, 57, 58

W

Wagner, Martin, 137, 141, 142
Water resources
  Amazon basin, 115–117, 123–124
  China, 170, 173–177
  Middle East, 90, 91
  threatened by drought, 32, 86–87, 90, 91
  threatened by rising water levels, 35, 98–99, 100, 105, 123–124, 174
  warming, 23–24, 47, 104, 117–118
  See also Sea level rises
Watt-Cloutier, Sheila, 135–137, 138, 140, 142–143
Wealthy nations. *See* Rich nations
Web of life. *See* Ecosystems, threats
White House Council on Environmental Quality (CEQ), 68–72
White House executive policy
  international non-cooperation, 56, 58, 63, 64, 137, 166
  science manipulation/disinformation, 61, 67–72

Whitman, Christine Todd, 72

Wildlife, African, 86

Wind energy, 204, 207

See also Renewable energy

Working Groups, Intergovernmental Panel on Climate Change, 27–28

World Agroforestry Centre-ICRAF, 184, 186–187

World Food Programme (WFP), 93

World history, 30

World Meteorological Organization (WMO), 27

World Wildlife Fund (WWF), 109

Y

Yemen, 91

Z

Zambia, 85–86

Zhang, David, 30

Zimbabwe, 87